About the Author

Søren Kierkegaard (1813–1855) continues to exercise a wide influence on philosophy, literature, and theology. After a youth spent cultivating the lifestyle of a Romantic aesthete, he finished his studies at the University of Copenhagen with the dissertation *On the Concept of Irony*. Many of his books were published under exotic pseudonyms, and explored different dimensions of life outside Christianity. These include *Either/Or*, *Fear and Trembling*, and *The Concept of Anxiety*. He also wrote a number of more directly devotional works, including *Works of Love* and the collection *Spiritual Writings* (edited by George Pattison), but in the last years of his life he attacked the established Church in a series of polemical leaflets.

THE
PRESENT AGE

Also by Søren Kierkegaard

Works of Love
(Translated by Howard and Edna Hong)

Spiritual Writings
(Translated by George Pattison)

THE
PRESENT AGE

On the Death of Rebellion

Søren Kierkegaard

*Also Includes "Of the Difference Between
a Genius and an Apostle"*

Translated by

ALEXANDER DRU

With an Introduction by

WALTER KAUFMANN

HARPER**PERENNIAL** MODERN**THOUGHT**

NEW YORK ● LONDON ● TORONTO ● SYDNEY ● NEW DELHI ● AUCKLAND

HARPER**PERENNIAL** 🅧 MODERN**THOUGHT**

These essays were originally published, together with a third essay, by Oxford University Press under the title *The Present Age and Two Minor Ethico-Religious Treatises* in 1940, and are here reprinted by arrangement with the translator, Alexander Dru.

HarperCollins books may be purchased for educational, business, or sales promotional use. For information, please write: Special Markets Department, HarperCollins Publishers, 10 East 53rd Street, New York, NY 10022.

First Harper Torchbook edition published 1962 by Harper & Row, Publishers.

First Harper Perennial Modern Thought edition published 2010.

Designed by Justin Dodd

Library of Congress Cataloging-in-Publication Data is available upon request.

ISBN 978-0-06-199003-8 (Harper Perennial Modern Thought edition)

14   OV/RRD   10 9 8 7 6 5 4

Contents

Introduction by Walter Kaufmann   ix

The Present Age   1
Of the Difference Between a Genius and an Apostle   63

Introduction

It is one of the characteristics of the present age that books of the previous century are reissued with more or less—usually less—learned prefaces. The point is partly that the new edition should have something new in it; partly that the reader should be told what a great classic will confront him when he is done with the preface. The reader wants to be reassured that he is not going to waste his time. And he is also supposed to be anxious to know what he should think of the book—which is another way of saying that he is supposed to be afraid of having to think for himself, though this is after all the only kind of thinking there is. In Kierkegaard's words, in *The Present Age*, the reader must be reassured that 'something is going to happen,' for 'ours is the age of advertisement and publicity.' Indeed, the preface is expected to say *what* is going to happen—or, more precisely, which parts of what is about to happen may be safely forgotten, which points are memorable, and what observations about them should be remembered for use in conversation.

The fact that a man wrote books to attack these and other features of the present age and that he strained to be offensive, especially to parsons and professors, provides no protection whatsoever. For it is also one of the features of the present age not to take offence, if only the author's reputation is above question and one can be sure that reading him is not a waste of time. If the dust has not yet settled on his books, of course, it is quite safe to say he is offensive, or his works are in bad taste or, better yet, completely 'unsound' (as Freud's writings were said to be early in the twentieth century)—and therefore not to read them. But once a writer has arrived and reached the stage where other men write prefaces for posthumous editions of his books, it would hardly be sophisticated to consider him offensive. Voltaire has to be placed in his historic context, Mephistopheles 'works' in the play or in the poet's gradual development, and Nietzsche stimulated this or that development. To be offended by them would be quite as prudish as taking offence at Aristophanes or Joyce. Why, they are classics!

One of the most important functions of a preface is to forestall any possibility that after all some wayward reader, here or there, should be offended. Dates must remind such readers that the author is long dead and that the book is old. Names must assure him that the author's thoughts were influenced by other writers and thus links in a development—not really, as one might think on reading them, deliberately nasty. And, of course, there should be many references to

'anticipations,' lest the reader take some statement as a prov-
ocation instead of considering it as the grandfather of someone else's proposition, which may be quite dull, and even
a great-grandfather, if only the later author is respectable
when the preface is written.

How Kierkegaard might have enjoyed this comedy! Yet
his laughter would hardly have been free of bitterness. His
laughter rarely was. And in this case, there is abundant
reason for sorrow. His name is now a name to conjure with,
bandied about with great abandon both at cocktail parties
and in books and articles that are as nourishing as cocktail
party fare; but his central aspirations are almost invariably
ignored, and even those who notice them often give reasons
why the things that mattered most to him may be dismissed
as really of no account.

That he is so often presented as a saturnine thinker, as
sedate as the German existentialists, might have amused
him, and he might have written a neat parody of prefaces in
which there is no glimpse of his own sense of humour—not
even a hint that something funny is ahead. But could he
have smiled at the ever-growing literature that reassures us
that he was, even if he did not know it, really a humanist?

Since Jaspers first dismissed Kierkegaard's 'forced Christianity' as well as Nietzsche's 'forced anti-Christianity' as rel-
atively unimportant, lesser commentators have ornamented
this notion with appalling metaphors: 'Kierkegaard satisfied this need [for metaphysics] within the withered bosom

of Christian dogmatics—a satisfaction which ultimately harmed rather than enhanced the genius of his thought. But by Nietzsche's time this bosom was dry, and Nietzsche gratified his penchant for a well-rounded . . . ' There is no need to continue. In this interpretation Kierkegaard winds up as a man who painfully groped his way 'toward a point of view which is largely identical with the insights of orthodox Hinduism, of primitive Indian Buddhism, and of . . . Zen,' but who also was a humanist.

Actually, of course, Kierkegaard's religious existence culminated in a grand *Attack on Christendom* and the refusal to accept the sacraments from any ordained minister. He wanted the last sacraments from a layman but, denied this wish, died without them, hoping soon 'to sit upon the clouds and sing: Hallelujah, hallelujah, hallelujah!' He did not doubt the divine grace but felt that his church had betrayed Christ by not sufficiently insisting on his authority and the fundamental offence—what Paul had called the *skandalon* and what Kierkegaard often called the absurdity—of Christian teaching. Would he have been amused by the rarely questioned notion that one can have one's Kierkegaard and go to church, too—and that Kierkegaard must naturally be assimilated to such other revolutionary spirits as Marx, Freud, and Nietzsche?

Those who consider him a humanist and those who think that the commitment called for in his writings is in essence the commitment to be either Protestant, Catholic, or Jew, and to support the church, or possibly the temple, of your choice, turn Kierkegaard into the very thing he most consistently opposed: an apostle of reassurance. These disciples, who often resent all criticism of the master and make much of their great admiration for him, really betray him with a kiss.

Indeed, the present age is the age of Judas. Who would stand up against Christ and be counted His opponent? Who openly rejects the claims of the New Testament? Who lets his Yea be yea, 'Nay, nay: for whatsoever is more than these cometh of evil'? Certainly not the apologists who simply ignore what gives offence or, when this is not feasible, offer 'interpretations' instead of saying Nay. To be sure, it is not literally with a kiss that Christ is betrayed in the present age: today one betrays with an interpretation. The interpretation may be bold, extremely bold, as long as it is offered as an interpretation and the reader is reassured that the original text is profound and beautiful.

This, of course, is not a pleasant way of saying something that could easily be put a little more politely. Why speak of betrayal and, worse yet, of Judas? Because Kierkegaard himself remarked in *The Sickness unto Death* that 'he who first invented the notion of defending Christianity in Christendom is *de facto* Judas No. 2; he also betrays with a kiss' (218).

But surely, good sir, you must see that it is quite a different proposition in the mouth of Kierkegaard, more than a century ago, than in a preface written in the present age! Besides, he spoke of Danes while you—you are offensive. You attack men whom you should applaud: fine, decent men who do their best to make the gospel inoffensive, reading into it an ethic that you ought to welcome.

Some men who think thus have no hesitation about putting Kierkegaard's name on their banners, along with many other fashionable names, certain that positions other than their own deserve not only criticism but strong language; but their own views, well, are different and plainly should be privileged. And anyone who fails to see that simply is not nice. It is easy to see this point—at least after one has been requested to behold it from a hundred angles: every time it is the speaker, or the writer, whose outlook is clearly an exception. Against A and B and C and D one might have used far stronger language if one only had admitted that, of course, X is superior to all criticism. Next time it is Y or Z or A or B. The idea is always the same: criticism is a splendid thing, as long as we are spared. And fashionable writers, such as Kierkegaard, were marvellous—oh, simply marvellous—when they made fun of Hegel (as who did not?) or of all kinds of Danish theologians (of whom, but for him, we should not even know the names) or of 'the public' (which plainly means the others and not us); but if anyone made remarks at our expense, he either was badly mistaken and may therefore be ignored, if not abhorred, or, now that his fame has passed the point where that was feasible, he either did not mean it or that aspect of his thought was marginal and clearly should be disregarded.

Kierkegaard is fine, says the present age, provided only he is cut and dried a little, milked of his unpleasant venom, and—in one word—bowdlerized. But in the present age one no longer literally changes texts; instead, to say it once more, one betrays with interpretations. It may seem that this procedure is not new: some liberals consider Paul a pioneer of this insidious method; others, yet more radical, regard the Gospels as examples. However that may be, what is new is the scholarly approach or rather the display of dubious scholarship: the invocation of a multitude of names of little relevance, the desiccated prose that in its deathly pallor leans on pointless footnotes, and the striking fact that the perversion is accomplished without passion. Life and death are utterly out of the picture as is any question of a mission: we breathe classroom air or, yet more often, the dust of the journal shelves.

But, good sir! the present age replies; you cannot hope to excuse your bad manners by appealing to Kierkegaard; or do you really fancy that he could have approved of a preface that makes fun of prefaces? After all, he was a great human being—witness the large literature about him, which surely proves this, even if we have not read it—and it stands to reason that he would not have been guilty of lack of respect for fellow scholars. Classroom air and dusty journal shelves! Assuredly he'd never have gone that far.

Sancta simplicitas! The present-day Judases no longer *know* what they betray, any more than they know what they like: what they know is only the preface written by another hand, the lecture given by a parson or professor, the interpretation of the well-known critic. Of course, one is sure of one's likes and dislikes—much surer than one might be if one really knew the texts. One knows that Kierkegaard was a precursor of this and that, but not his mordant humour, nor the fantastic comedy he played out with his pseudonyms who attacked each other, keeping literary Denmark guessing whether these books with their tangled prefaces and postscripts by pseudonyms and editors were written by one, two, or more writers. Could he have endured a preface to a posthumous edition of *The Present Age* that did *not* ridicule prefaces and the whole stuffy establishment that he attacked, not only in *The Present Age*? He abhorred the modern apotheosis of good taste.

What makes *The Present Age* and *The Difference Between a Genius and an Apostle* important is not so much that the former essay anticipates Heidegger and the latter, Barth: it would be more accurate to say that Heidegger's originality is widely overestimated, and that many things he says at great length in his highly obscure German were said earlier by various writers who had made the same points much more elegantly, and that some of these writers, including Kierkegaard, were known to Heidegger. Why should Kierkegaard's significance depend on someone else's, quite especially when many points that others copied from him may be wrong? And are his observations about 'the public,' which remind the modern

German reader of long-winded 'philosophical' discussions of *das Man*, and American readers of even more long-winded, but also more intelligible, discussions of 'other-directedness' really very important? Surely, they are witty in a rather innocuous way: like statistics about Protestant, Catholic, and Jew, they allow us to smile and feel superior. Gratitude repays this favour by calling the author a remarkable psychologist who anticipated twentieth century insights.

Much of what Kierkegaard is too often praised for is not really very profound or beautiful but rather entertaining and amusing. And few writers protested more than he did against submerging challenges to our faith and morals in effusive talk about what is profound and beautiful. Sometimes he used these very words; at other times he juxtaposed what he called an aesthetic orientation with an ethico-religious outlook. One of his best-known and best books, *Fear and Trembling*, is directed in large measure against those who read the Bible from an 'aesthetic' point of view, admiring Abraham along with the beautiful story which tells of his readiness to sacrifice his son, although the readers would abhor as a religious fanatic any contemporary who resolved to act like Abraham. Kierkegaard may have misread the story, but it is perfectly clear that he was nauseated by prolonged talk about the profound and beautiful when the one question needful was how we should live.

He once wrote an essay with the title: *Has a Man the Right to let himself be put to Death for the Truth?* Walter Lowrie's translation of it was published in the same volume with the original English edition of *The Present Age,* but is omitted in the paperback reprint. The essay is exceedingly prolix and takes its time to conclude that 'a *man* (unlike God) has not the right to let himself be put to death for the truth'; for he should be 'lovingly *concerned for others,* for those who, if one is put to death, must become guilty of putting one to death.' In the long reflections that lead up to this conclusion, there is a passage that sums up succinctly (for Kierkegaard) a point also found in *Fear and Trembling* and, for that matter, throughout his works:

'The parson (collectively understood) does indeed preach about those glorious ones who sacrificed their lives for the truth. As a rule the parson is justified in assuming that there is no one present in the church who could entertain the notion of venturing upon such a thing. When he is sufficiently assured of this by reason of the private knowledge he has of the congregation as its pastor, he preaches glibly, declaims vigorously, and wipes away the sweat. If on the following day one of those strong and silent men . . . were to visit the parson at his house announcing himself as one whom the parson had carried away by his eloquence, so that he had now resolved to sacrifice his life for the truth—what would the parson say? He would address him thus: "Why, merciful Father in heaven! How did such an idea ever occur to you? Travel, divert yourself, take a laxative" . . .'

A writer who so persistently distinguished between what he called an aesthetic approach and what we might call an existential approach should not be approached and discussed on the aesthetic plane, as he usually is. All talk not only of profundity and beauty but also of influences and anticipations remains on the aesthetic plain. And it is more in Kierkegaard's spirit to take offence and to disagree than to defend him and betray him with a kiss.

Walter Lowrie had much more feeling for Kierkegaard than most commentators, and there is nobody from whom one can learn more about Kierkegaard. In his big book on *Kierkegaard* (293), Lowrie remarked: 'all the trends of his thinking find their ultimate and most adequate expression in this work [*Concluding Unscientific Postscript*], in the *Literary Review*, and in *The Book about Adler*,' all of which Kierkegaard wrote in his early thirties. Later (on p. 365), Lowrie makes clear that he is referring to 'the latter part of . . . *A Literary Review*, published in 1846,' that is, to those pages which are known in English under the title, *The Present Age*. And those who have read Lowrie's complete translation of *On Authority and Revelation: The Book on Adler* will agree that it contains passages that are quite exceptionally important for an understanding of Kierkegaard; that the book is quite exceptionally verbose even for Kierkegaard; and that he did well when, instead of publishing the whole manuscript, he polished for publication only the crucial passages, which he issued under the title: *Of the Difference between a Genius and an Apostle*. In sum, the unusual significance of the two essays brought together in the present volume is that, for better or for worse, many of the central trends of Kierkegaard's thinking find superb expression in them.

Dear reader! Kierkegaard might say; pray be so good as to look for *my* thinking in these pages—not for Nietzsche's, Barth's, or Heidegger's, de Tocqueville's, or anyone else's. And least of all, dear reader, fancy that if you should find that a few others have said, too, what I have said, that makes it true. Oh, least of all suppose that numbers can create some small presumption of the truth of an idea. What I would have you ask, dear reader, is not whether I am in good company: to be candid, I should have much preferred to stand alone, as a matter of principle; and besides I do not like the men with whom the kissing Judases insist on lumping me. Rather ask yourself if I am right. And if I am not, then for heaven's sake do not pretend that I am, emphasizing a few points that are reasonable, even if not central to my thought, while glossing over those ideas which you do not like, or which, in retrospect, are plainly wrong, although I chose to take my stand on them. Do not forget, dear reader, that I made a point of taking for my motto (in my *Philosophical Scraps*): 'Better well hung than ill wed!'

Alas! he might add if he saw the *present* age; who remembers that motto? Of course, it is not easy to find. When I published my *Scraps*—or *Crumbs,* if you prefer—the motto could hardly be missed because it stared the reader in the face if he but turned the title page. But when these *Scraps* appeared in the *present* age, they had to be made respectable: they were called *Philosophical*

Fragments (which is almost as dignified as *Opus postumum*) and began, naturally, with a long and solemn preface. Wedged between that and my own text, the motto was easily overlooked. And now there is even a triple-decker edition of the *Fragments* in which my lowly *Scraps* are sandwiched between two prefaces and a long commentary. My book takes up little more than one third of that, let us hope, definitive edition: and who is likely to find the motto, now lost somewhere in the middle? Of course, it is a fine commentary, and the reader who studies it will note that I misquoted Shakespeare, to whom I attributed the motto—presumably because I had read my Shakespeare in German. A good point, surely well worth making. The commentator is a scholar and knows his job, far better than most writers of prefaces. But the pity of it is that nobody remembers that I, Søren Kierkegaard, would rather be 'well hung than ill wed.' Almost everybody who writes or talks about me is concerned to make me the victim of some unpleasant mesalliance, and by now I have been ill wed scores of times. What a relief it would be to be well hung!

In the present age, of course, it would be out of the question to go as far as that. We could not possibly accommodate the author's own wishes when writing a preface to one of his books. But perhaps it would not be absolutely necessary to defy his spirit *in toto,* as he might have said. Let us at least try to meet him half way.

Suppose, by a bold flight of the imagination, that an author said in 1846 that in the present age a revolution is unthinkable. Suppose further, if you can, that in 1847 seven Catholic cantons secede in Switzerland and are forced in a short war to return to the federation; that in 1848 a revolution in France overthrows the monarchy and establishes a republic, while revolutions also sweep Germany and Austria and Italy; Denmark annexes Schleswig-Holstein (taking advantage of the fighting in Germany), a revolt flares up in Hungary, wars sweep through Italy, Prussian and Austrian troops expel the Danes from Schleswig-Holstein, the Communists in Paris rise against the new republic and are beaten down in bloody street fights, the Emperor has to flee Vienna, more bloody revolts are fought out in Paris, the Emperor of Austria is forced to abdicate in favour of his nephew—all in 1848. And then imagine things proceeding in a kindred spirit during 1849. But our author said in 1846 that 'in the present age a rebellion is, of all things, the most unthinkable.' Does it tax the sense of irony too far if we imagine further that, a century after the author made his statement, interpreters pretend that he made no mistake at all and actually tell us that he 'perceived the deeper trends and foresaw' not, to be sure, what was just about to happen (they don't deign to mention any of the events just recited) but—what shall we say?—the future?

Of course, one could consider extenuating circumstances. After all, he might well have perceived the deeper trends even if he did not foresee the future; and a good deal of what he said about the present age in 1846 might still be true of the second half of the twentieth century. Some historians might even argue that the revolutions of 1848 were peculiar in some ways and lacked the profundity of the French Revolution. If our author was right in spite of apparent evidence to the contrary, then it is not he that deserves to be well hung but rather his interpreters who have failed to come to grips with the evidence. And if a posthumous preface to one of his books ought to breathe a little of his spirit, it is not needful after all that it should turn against him; but it is entirely proper that it should attempt to rescue him from his friends. By all means, read his book—only read it truly, and do not assume that any preface (whether this one or another) can all but take its place.

The case is similar to that of another so-called existentialist who all but borrowed Kierkegaard's title and published a little book on 'The Spiritual Situation of the Age,' as volume 1,000 in a popular series. Two years later, when his book had already gone through four editions, the Nazis came to power in Germany. Many people still cite it as a penetrating essay that perceived the deeper trends, even if it did not foresee what was just about to happen. And if the author considered Freud at least as dangerous as Hitler, he at least had the consistency to reiterate in 1950, in a volume on 'Reason and Anti-Reason in Our Age,' that Marxism and psychoanalysis are the two great representatives of anti-reason in the present age. His book, too, *was* quite perceptive in some ways; but surely his analysis 'of the Age' has its comic dimension, too, if one considers when it appeared. Yet writers on existentialism never tire of paying tribute to the supposedly marvellous manner in which Kierkegaard made fun of Hegel, while they would not dream of ridiculing existentialists.

Scores of professors have made fun of the supposedly so professorial Hegel, though they consider it exceedingly bad taste to make fun of Professor Jaspers, who wrote the two books just mentioned, of Professor Heidegger, whom Kierkegaard would surely have found funnier than Hegel, or of Kierkegaard himself. But they know not what they do. They are simply ignorant of the agonies of Hegel's life, of the gradual decline into insanity of Hegel's onetime roommate, Hölderlin; of his sister, as close to him as any human being, who lived on the verge of madness till she finally fell over the precipice; of his illegitimate, pre-marital son who brought heartbreak into Hegel's life again and again. Hegel's supposed remoteness from life and from his own existential situation is proverbial, and he is considered fair game, however unfair the dig; but if Kierkegaard made ridiculous errors, we must look the other way and pretend nothing happened.

When *The Present Age* first appeared in English, complete with preface and footnotes, there was no mention at all of politics or actual revolutions, and the author's statement that 'In the present age a rebellion is, of all things, the most unthinkable' was not glossed. All one was told of 1848 was that Kierkegaard did not really 'speak in his own voice . . .

until after the "metamorphosis" [?] of 1848. But he was already aware of it.' O his prophetic soul!

His *Misundelse* was translated, as it still is, as *ressentiment*. A footnote explained that this French term was 'first
used forty years later by Nietzsche to describe the same process,' and went on to cite—not Nietzsche but a French book,
L'homme du Ressentiment by Max Scheller. Scheler (Scheller
was a printer's error) was, of course, a German philosopher
who wrote in German (even if some of his essays were later
translated into other languages), and his conception of *ressentiment* did not by any means agree completely with Nietzsche's, who had preceded him by roughly thirty years. Above
all, Nietzsche did not 'describe the same process' that Kierkegaard describes in *The Present Age;* Nietzsche had found
ressentiment in the heart of Christianity, he had found it
creating the values of the New Testament. A detailed comparison of Kierkegaard, Nietzsche, and Scheler might be re-
warding; but not giving us the original word at all and not
rendering it literally, say, as envy (the best German translation says *Neid,* which is envy), but rather with a technical
term from another man's philosophy, forestalls comparison,
analysis, and needful thought. Indeed, a later essay claims
that Kierkegaard, in *The Present Age*, 'forestalls one of the
most famous passages in Nietzsche.' One may wonder how
an author in 1846 could have forestalled a passage written
forty years later—written and not forestalled after all—but
such a claim at least forestalls doubts about Kierkegaard's

prophetic powers: even if he neither foresaw nor forestalled the revolutions of 1848, he at least forestalled a passage in Nietzsche.

Kierkegaard is safely dead and therefore had the right to be as nasty as he pleased and to make fun of the professors of his day and of the foibles of his age. He can even count on the applause of those, a hundred years later, who walk in the footsteps not of Kierkegaard but of the men at whom he laughed. But to make fun of them—well, don't you see that in the present age that simply isn't done because it would be in bad taste? We must admire Kierkegaard for having done what, if anyone today presumed to do it, we should find detestable. Just so, we must admire Abraham and condemn those who imitate him. To be sure, that was the very attitude which Kierkegaard opposed throughout his literary work. But if anyone should take Kierkegaard seriously, which simply would not be genteel, instead of admiring him, which is the thing to do, he would be told: 'How did such an idea ever occur to you? Travel, divert yourself, take a laxative.' No, not really that: such a humorous way of putting it is much too Kierkegaardian. He would just be told that it was in horrible taste.

What, then, makes *The Present Age* worth reading, if it merely forestalled a passage in Nietzsche but not the revolutions of 1848? That kind of question, so characteristic of the present age, is here on trial. It is contested by the whole literary existence of Kierkegaard. 'Worth reading' and 'what should I get out of reading this?' are phrases that bring to mind Nietzsche's remark: 'Another century of readers—and the spirit itself will stink.'

Read for the flavour, chew the phrases, enjoy the humour, feel the offence when you are attacked, don't ignore the author's blunders, but don't fail to look for your own shortcomings as well: then the book will make you a better man than you were before. But if you should find it too strenuous to read for the joy and pain of an encounter with a human being who, exasperated with himself, his age, and you, does not—let's face it—like you, then leave the book alone and do not look for marvellous anticipations!

To be sure, *The Present Age,* which formed part of a long book review published over Kierkegaard's own name, is conclusive proof that he meant it when he said in one of his most important pseudonymous books, *Fear and Trembling,* that 'What our age lacks is not reflection but passion' (53); and probably he himself also believed that 'the conclusions of passion are the only reliable ones . . .' (109). Surely, the first of these statements, however understandable in the Victorian era, is ridiculously false in the *present* age; our time lacks both, but it certainly does not need any depreciation of reflection. And the second statement cannot be fully excused by the age in which it was written. *The Present Age* refutes those who would dissociate Kierkegaard from these pseudonymous utterances, and it shows *why* he thought as he did, what provoked his anger, what he fought.

There are other places in his books where the same ideas find expression. In the 'Diapsalmata,' for example, early in *Either/Or,* he says, though not over his own name: 'Let others complain that the age is wicked; my complaint is that it is paltry; for it lacks passion. Men's thoughts are thin and flimsy . . . The thoughts of their hearts are too paltry to be sinful . . . This is the reason my soul always turns back to the Old Testament and to Shakespeare. I feel that those who speak there are at least human beings: they hate, they love, they murder their enemies . . . they sin.'

Surely, one can understand Kierkegaard and sympathize with him without altogether agreeing. Perhaps the revolutions of 1848 *were* paltry compared with the French Revolution and with the upheavals of the *present* age—still it remains a fact that many thousands risked and lost their lives for their beliefs. And a hundred years later it had become rather plain that the conclusions of passion are by no means reliable, and that millions may lose their lives fighting for beliefs so utterly unfounded and inhuman that not even such a bloody sacrifice can hallow them. The reader who wants nothing but the truth should not read Kierkegaard's *The Present Age*—or other classics. But those who would know Kierkegaard, the intensely religious humorist, the irrepressibly witty critic of his age and ours, can do no better than to begin with this book.

The essay on *The Difference between a Genius and an Apostle* also shows that the extreme authoritarianism implicit in

Fear and Trembling represents the author's considered view, and that he really considered blasphemous any suggestion that, confronted with what purports to be God's word, we should first 'see whether the content . . . is divine, in which case we will accept it. . . .' Kierkegaard revered Abraham for the unflinching authoritarianism and the ethic of utterly blind obedience that he attributed to him, however mistakenly. He admired Abraham for not looking at the content of the commandment to sacrifice his son, and for not concluding that it was not divine and could not come from God. In *Fear and Trembling,* Kierkegaard added: 'If faith does not make it a holy act to be willing to murder one's son, then let the same condemnation be pronounced upon Abraham as upon every other man' (41).

In *The Difference Between a Genius and an Apostle* and in *The Present Age* we find the heart of Kierkegaard. It is not innocuous, not genteel, not comfortable. He does not invite the reader to relax and have a little laugh with him at the expense of other people or at his own foibles. Kierkegaard deliberately challenges the reader's whole existence.

Nor does he merely challenge our *existence;* he also questions some ideas that had become well entrenched in his time and that are even more characteristic of the *present* age. Kierkegaard insists, for example, that Christianity was from the start essentially authoritarian—not just that the Catholic Church was, or that Calvin was, or Luther, or, regrettably, most of the Christian churches, but that Christ was—and is.

Indeed, though Kierkegaard was, and wished to be, an individual, and even said that on his tombstone he would like no other epitaph than 'That Individual,' his protest against his age was centered in his lament over the loss of authority.

In the present age it is fashionable to lump Jesus with the prophets and the Buddha, with Confucius, Lao-tze, and Zen, with the mystics and Spinoza—sometimes even with the French Enlightenment and Freud—as if everybody who had been at all attractive must, of course, have been a humanist, and only Hitler, Stalin, Calvin, and the Catholic Church had been authoritarian. It is axiomatic that Jesus' teaching was the most attractive teaching ever uttered, and any suggestion that it was not is branded as vilification. Only if the content was divine—or rather what the present age considers worthy of this epithet—may any teaching be ascribed to Jesus. The appalling possibility that Kierkegaard insisted we consider was that God's teaching might not agree completely with the predilections and the conscience of the present age.

If it were really axiomatic that God could never contravene our conscience and our reason—if we could be sure that he must share our moral judgments—would not God become superfluous as far as ethics is concerned? A mere redundancy? If God is really to make a moral difference in our lives, Kierkegaard insists, we must admit that he might go against our reason and our conscience, and that he should still be obeyed.

That, of course, is merely one aspect of Kierkegaard, though certainly one of the most important. But even if we come to conclude in the end that many of his ideas are untenable, or downright horrible, that does not mean that he was not 'worth reading.' The same consideration applies to Plato and Dante; and those who do not read the Scriptures after the manner of Judas might even agree that it applies to the Bible, too. Indeed, it is worth asking whether this is not a feature that is more often found than not found in the greatest books. They do not mainly seek to add to our knowledge: they do not disdain shocking us because what they most want to do is change us.[*]

—Walter Kaufmann

---

[*] For a more detailed discussion of Kierkegaard, see Walter Kaufmann, *From Shakespeare to Existentialism* (Anchor Books paperback), especially Chapter 10; but also some of the other passages listed in the Index.

The Present Age

Our age is essentially one of understanding and reflection, without passion, momentarily bursting into enthusiasm, and shrewdly relapsing into repose.

If we had statistical tables of the consumption of intelligence from generation to generation as we have for spirits, we should be astounded at the enormous amount of scruple and deliberation consumed by small, well-to-do families living quietly, and at the amount which the young, and even children, use. For just as the children's crusade may be said to typify the Middle Ages, precocious children are typical of the present age. In fact one is tempted to ask whether there is a single man left ready, for once, to commit an outrageous folly.

Nowadays not even a suicide kills himself in desperation. Before taking the step he deliberates so long and so carefully that he literally chokes with thought. It is even questionable whether he ought to be called a suicide, since it is really thought which takes his life. He does not die *with* deliberation but *from* deliberation.

It would therefore be very difficult to prosecute the present generation in view of its legal quibbles: in fact, its ability, virtuosity and good sense consists in trying to reach a judgement and a decision without ever going as far as action. If one may say of the revolutionary period that it runs wild, one would have to say of the present that it runs badly. Between them, the individual and his generation always bring each other to a standstill, with the result that the prosecuting attorney would find it next to impossible to get any fact admitted—because nothing really happens. To judge from innumerable indications, one would conclude that something quite exceptional had either just happened or was just about to happen. Yet any such conclusion would be quite wrong. Indications are, indeed, the only achievements of the age; and its skill and inventiveness in constructing fascinating illusions, its bursts of enthusiasm, using as a deceitful escape some projected change of form, must be rated as high in the scale of cleverness and of the negative use of strength as the passionate, creative energy of the revolution in the corresponding scale of energy. But the present generation, wearied by its chimerical efforts, relapses into complete indolence. Its condition is that of a man who has only fallen asleep towards morning: first of all come great dreams, then a feeling of laziness, and finally a witty or clever excuse for remaining in bed.

However well-meaning and strong the individual man may be (if he could only use his strength), he still has not the passion to be able to tear himself from the coils and seductive uncertainty of reflection. Nor do his surroundings supply the events or produce the general enthusiasm necessary in order to free him. Instead of coming to his help, his *milieu* forms around him a negative intellectual opposition, which juggles for a moment with a deceptive prospect, only to deceive him in the end by pointing to a brilliant way out of the difficulty—by showing him that the shrewdest thing of all is to do nothing. For at the bottom of the tergiversation of the present age is *vis inertiae,* and every one without passion congratulates himself upon being the first to discover it, and so becomes cleverer still. During the revolution arms were distributed freely, just as during the Crusades the insignia of the exploit were bestowed upon men, but nowadays people are supplied with rules of careful conduct and ready-reckoners to facilitate judgement. If a generation were given the diplomatic task of postponing any action in such a way as to make it seem as if something were just about to happen, then we should have to admit that our age had performed as remarkable a feat as the revolutionary age. Let any one try forgetting all he knows of the age and its actual relativity which is so enhanced by familiarity, and then arrive, as it were, from another world: if he were then to read a book or an article in the papers, or merely to speak to some passer-by, his impression would be: 'Good heavens, something is going to happen tonight—or perhaps something happened the night before last.'

A revolutionary age is an age of action; ours is the age of advertisement and publicity. Nothing ever happens but there is immediate publicity everywhere. In the present age a rebellion is, of all things, the most unthinkable. Such an expression of strength would seem ridiculous to the calculating intelligence of our times. On the other hand a political virtuoso might bring off a feat almost as remarkable. He might write a manifesto suggesting a general assembly at which people should decide upon a rebellion, and it would be so carefully worded that even the censor would let it pass. At the meeting itself he would be able to create the impression that his audience had rebelled, after which they would all go quietly home—having spent a very pleasant evening. Among the young men of today a profound and prodigious learning is almost unthinkable; they would find it ridiculous. On the other hand a scientific virtuoso might draw up a subscription form outlining an all-embracing system which he purposed to write and, what is more, in such a way that the reader would feel he had already read the system; for the age of encyclopaedists, when men wrote gigantic folios with unremitting pains, is gone. Now is the turn of those light-weight encyclopaedists who, *en passant,* deal with all the sciences and the whole of existence. Equally unthinkable among the young men of today is a truly religious renunciation of the world, adhered to with daily self-denial. On the other hand almost any theological student is capable of something far more wonderful. He could found a society with the sole object of saving all those who are lost. The age of great and good actions is past, the present is the age of anticipation when even recognition is received in advance. No one is satisfied with doing something definite, every one wants to feel flattered by reflection with the illusion of having discovered at the very least a new continent. Like a young man who decides to work for his examination in all earnest from September 1st, and in order to strengthen his resolution decides to take a holiday during August, so the present generation seems—though this is decidedly more difficult to understand—to have made a solemn resolution that the next generation should set to work seriously, and in order to avoid disturbing or delaying the next generation, the present attends to—the banquets. Only there is a difference: the young man understands himself in the light-heartedness of youth, whereas our generation is serious—even at banquets.

There is no more action or decision in our day than there is perilous delight in swimming in shallow waters. But just as a grown-up, struggling delightedly in the waves, calls to those younger than himself: 'Come on, jump in quickly'—the decision in existence, so to speak (of course it is in the individual), calls out to the young who are not as yet worn out by over-reflective thought or overburdened by the illusions of reflective thought: Come on, leap cheerfully, even if it means a light-hearted leap, so long as it is decisive. If you are capable of being a man, then danger and the harsh judgement of existence on your thoughtlessness will help you to become one.

If the jewel which every one desired to possess lay far out on a frozen lake where the ice was very thin, watched over by the danger of death, while, closer in, the ice was perfectly safe, then in a passionate age the crowds would applaud the courage of the man who ventured out, they would tremble for him and with him in the danger of his decisive action, they would grieve over him if he were drowned, they would make a god of him if he secured the prize. But in an age without passion, in a reflective age, it would be otherwise. People would think each other clever in agreeing that it was unreasonable and not even worth while to venture so far out. And in this way they would transform *daring and enthusiasm* into a *feat of skill,* so as to do something, for after all 'something must be done.' The crowds would go out to watch from a safe place, and with the eyes of connoisseurs appraise the accomplished skater who could skate almost to the very edge (i.e. as far as the ice was still safe and the danger had not yet begun) and then turn back. The most accomplished skater would manage to go out to the furthermost point and then perform a still more dangerous-looking run, so as to make the spectators hold their breath and say: 'Ye Gods! How mad; he is risking his life.' But look, and you will see that his skill was so astonishing that he managed to turn back just in time, while the ice was perfectly safe and there was still no danger. As at the theatre, the crowd would applaud and acclaim him, surge homeward with the heroic artist in their midst, to honour him with a magnificent banquet. For intelligence has got the upper hand to such an extent that it transforms the real task into an unreal trick and reality into a play. During the banquet admiration would reach its height. Now the proper relation between the admirer and the object of admiration is one in which the admirer is edified by the thought that he is a man like the hero, humbled by the thought that he is incapable of such great actions, yet morally encouraged to emulate him according to his powers; but where intelligence has got the upper hand the character of admiration is completely altered. Even at the height of the banquet, when the applause was loudest, the admiring guests would all have a shrewd notion that the action of the man who received all the honour was not really so extraordinary, and that only by chance was the gathering for him, since after all, with a little practice, every one could have done as much. Briefly, instead of being strengthened in their discernment and encouraged to do good, the guests would more probably go home with an even stronger predisposition to the most dangerous, if also the most respectable, of all diseases: to admire in public what is considered unimportant in private—since everything is made into a joke. And so, stimulated by a gush of admiration, they are all comfortably agreed that they might just as well admire themselves.

Formerly it was agreed that a man stood or fell by his actions; nowadays, on the contrary, every one idles about and comes off brilliantly with the help of a little reflection, knowing perfectly well what ought to be done. But what two people talking together, or the speakers at a meeting, understand perfectly presented to them as a thought or as an observation, they cannot understand at all in the form of action. If some one were to overhear what people said ought to be done, and then in a spirit of irony, and for no other reason, proceeded to act accordingly every one would be amazed. They would find it rash, yet as soon as they had talked it over they would find that it was just what should be done.

The present age with its sudden enthusiasms followed by apathy and indolence is very near the comic; but those who understand the comic see quite clearly that the comic is not where the present age imagines. Now satire, if it is to do a little good and not cause immeasurable harm, must be firmly based upon a consistent ethical view of life, a natural distinction which renounces the success of the moment; otherwise the cure will be infinitely worse than the disease. The really comic thing is that an age such as this should try to be witty and humorous; for that is most certainly the last and most acrobatic way out of the impasse. What, indeed, is there for an age of reflection and thought to defy with humour? For, being without passion, it has lost all feeling for the values of eros, for enthusiasm and sincerity in politics and religion, or for piety, admiration and domesticity in everyday life. But even if the vulgar laugh, life only mocks at the wit which knows no values. To be witty without possessing the riches of inwardness is like squandering money upon luxuries and dispensing with necessities, or, as the proverb says, like selling one's breeches to buy a wig. But an age without passion has no values, and everything is transformed into representational ideas. Thus there are certain remarks and expressions current which, though true and reasonable up to a point, are lifeless. On the other hand no hero, no lover, no thinker, no knight of the faith, no proud man, no man in despair would claim to have experienced them completely and personally. And just as one longs for the clink of real money after the crackle of bank-notes, one longs nowadays for a little originality. Yet what is more spontaneous than wit? It is more spontaneous, at least more surprising, even than the first bud of spring and the first tender shoots of grain. Why, even if spring came according to agreement it would still be spring, but wit upon agreement would be disgusting.

But, now, supposing that as a relief from feverish and sudden enthusiasms things went so far that wit, that divine accident—an additional favour which comes as a sign from the gods, from the mysterious source of the inexplicable, so that not even the wittiest of men dares to say: to-morrow, but adoringly says: when it pleases the gods—but supposing that wit were to be transformed into its shabbiest contrary, a trivial necessity, so that it became a profitable branch of trade to manufacture and make up and remake, and buy up old and new witticisms—what an epigram on a witty age!

In the end, therefore, money will be the one thing people will desire, which is moreover only representative, an abstraction. Nowadays a young man hardly envies anyone his gifts, his art, the love of a beautiful girl, or his fame; he only envies him his money. Give me money, he will say, and I am saved. But the young man will not run riot, he will not deserve what repentance repays. He would die with nothing to reproach himself with, and under the impression that if only he had had the money he might really have lived and might even have achieved something great.

After these general observations, and having compared the present age with the revolutionary age, it will be in order to go back to the dialectical and categorical definitions of the present age, regardless whether they are present at a given moment or not. We are concerned here with the 'how' of the age, and this 'how' must be defined from a universal standpoint, the final consequences of which can be reached by deduction, *a posse ad esse,* and verified by observation and experience *ab esse ad posse.*

As far as its significance is concerned it is, of course, possible that the work of reflection, which is the task before the present age, may ultimately be explained in a higher form of existence. As for its quality, there is no doubt that the individual resting in his reflection can be just as well-intentioned as a passionate man who has made his decision; and conversely there may be just as much excuse for the man whose passions run away with him as for a man whose fault is never apparent, though he is cleverly aware that he lets himself be deceived by his reflection. The results of reflection are both dangerous and unforeseeable because one can never tell whether the decision which saves a man from evil is reached after thorough consideration, or whether it is simply the exhaustion resulting from reflection which prevents him from doing wrong. One thing, however, is certain, an increased power of reflection like an increased knowledge only adds to man's affliction, and above all it is certain that for the individual as for the generation no task is more difficult than to escape from the temptations of reflection, simply because they are so dialectical and the result of one clever discovery may give the whole question a new turn, because at any moment reflection is capable of explaining everything quite differently and allowing one some way of escape; because at the last moment of a reflective decision reflection is capable of changing everything—after one has made far greater exertions than are necessary to get a man of character into the midst of things.

But these are only the excuses of reflection and the real position in reflection remains unchanged, for it is only altered *within* reflection. Even if a certain injustice is done to the present age when it is compared to a complete and closed period (the present age is still struggling with all the difficulties of 'becoming'), such a qualification is only a reflective qualification; and then, in return, its uncertainty is filled with *hope.*

A passionate tumultuous age will *overthrow everything, pull everything down;* but a revolutionary age, that is at the same time reflective and passionless, transforms that expression of strength into *a feat of dialectics: it leaves everything standing but cunningly empties it of significance. Instead of culminating in a rebellion it reduces the inward reality of all relationships to a reflective tension which leaves everything standing but makes the whole of life ambiguous: so that everything continues to exist factually whilst by a dialectical deceit,* privatissime, *it supplies a secret interpretation—that it does not exist.*

Morality is character, character is that which is engraved (χαράσσω); but the sand and the sea have no character and neither has abstract intelligence, for character is really inwardness. Immorality, as energy, is also character; but to be neither moral nor immoral is merely ambiguous, and ambiguity enters into life when the qualitative distinctions are weakened by a gnawing reflection. The revolt of the passions is elemental, the dissolution brought about by ambiguity is a silent sorites* that goes on night and day. The distinction between good and evil is enervated by a superficial, superior and theoretical knowledge of evil, and by a supercilious cleverness which is aware that goodness is neither appreciated nor worth while in this world, that it is tantamount to stupidity. No one is any longer carried away by the desire for the good to perform great things, no one is precipitated by

---

* A form of sophism leading by gradual steps from truth to absurdity.—Tr.

evil into atrocious sins, and so there is nothing for either the good or the bad to talk about, and yet for that very reason people gossip all the more, since ambiguity is tremendously stimulating and much more verbose than rejoicing over goodness or repentance over evil.

The springs of life, which are only what they are because of the qualitative differentiating power of passion, lose their elasticity. The distance separating a thing from its opposite in quality no longer regulates the inward relation of things. All inwardness is lost, and to that extent the relation no longer exists, or else forms a colourless cohesion. The negative law is this: opposites are unable to dispense with each other and unable to hold together. The positive law is that they are able to dispense with each other and are able to hold together or, stated positively: opposites are unable to dispense with each other because of the connexion between them. But when the inward relation is wanting another takes its place: a quality is no longer related to its contrary; instead, the partners both stand and observe each other and *the state of tension thus produced is really the end of the relationship.* For example, the admirer no longer cheerfully and happily acknowledges greatness, promptly expressing his appreciation, and then rebelling against its pride and arrogance. Nor is the relationship in any sense the opposite. The admirer and the object of admiration stand like two polite equals, and observe each other. A subject no longer freely honours his king or is angered at his ambition. To be a subject has come to mean something quite different; it means to be a *third party*. The subject ceases to have a position within the relationship; he has no direct relation to the king but simply becomes an observer and deliberately works out the problem; i.e. the relation of a subject to his king. For a time committee after committee is formed, so long, that is to say, as there are still people who passionately want to be what they ought to be; but in the end the whole age becomes a committee. A father no longer curses his son in anger, using all his parental authority, nor does a son defy his father, a conflict which might end in the inwardness of forgiveness; on the contrary, their relationship is irreproachable, for it is really in process of ceasing to exist, since they are no longer related to one another within the relationship; in fact it has become a problem in which the two partners observe each other as in a game, instead of having any relation to each other, and they note down each other's remarks instead of showing a firm devotion. More and more people renounce the quiet and modest tasks of life, that are so important and pleasing to God, in order to achieve something greater; in order to think over the relationships of life in a higher relationship till in the end the whole generation has become a representation, who represent . . . it is difficult to say *who;* and who think about these relationships . . . for *whose* sake it is not easy to discover. A disobedient youth is no longer in fear of his schoolmaster—the relation is rather one of indifference in which schoolmaster and pupil discuss how a good school should be run. To go to school no longer means to be in fear of the master, or merely to learn, but rather implies being interested in the problem of education. Again the differentiating relation of man to woman is never broken in an audaciously licentious manner; decency is observed in such a way that one can only describe these innocent borderline flirtations as trivial.

What in fact should one call such relationships? A tension, I think, is the best description, not, however, a tension which strains the forces to breaking-point, but rather a tension which exhausts life itself and the fire of that enthusiasm and inwardness which makes the fetters of dependance and the crown of dominion light, which makes the child's obedience and the father's authority joyful, the admiration of the subject and the exaltation of the great fearless, which gives recognized importance to the master and thus to the disciple occasion to learn, which unites woman's weakness and man's strength in the equal strength of devotion. As it is the relationships still exist but they lack the force which makes it possible for them to draw together in inwardness and unite in harmony. The relationship expresses its presence and its absence simultaneously, not completely but rather as though it were drawled out, half-awake and uninterruptedly.

Perhaps I can explain what I mean by a very simple illustration? I once knew a family who owned a grandfather clock whose works for some reason or other had got out of order. But the fault did not result in the spring suddenly unwinding, or in the chain breaking or in the hand ceasing to strike; on the contrary, it went on striking in a curiously abstract, though confusing, way. It did not strike twelve times at twelve o'clock and once at one o'clock, but struck once all through the day at regular intervals. It went on striking all day long but never gave a definite time.

The same applies to a state of exhausted tension: the relationship continues; something is expressed with an abstract continuity which prevents any real break, but although it must nevertheless be described as an expression of the relationship, the relationship is not only ambiguously expressed, it is almost meaningless.

It is this deceptive lull in the relationship which continues the relation as a fact; the danger is that it favours the cunning deprivations of reflection. Against a rebellion one can use force, and an obvious counterfeit has only to wait for its punishment; but dialectical complications are difficult to root out, and it requires even better ears to track down the stealthy movement of reflection along its secret and ambiguous path.

The established order of things continues to exist, but it is its ambiguity which satisfies our reflective and passionless age. No one, for example, wishes to do away with the power of the king, but if little by little it could be transformed into something purely fictitious every one would be quite prepared to cheer him. No one, for example, wishes to bring about the downfall of the eminent, but if distinction could be shown to be purely fictitious then every one would be prepared to admire it. In the same way people are quite prepared to leave the Christian terminology untouched, but they can surreptitiously interpolate that it involves no decisive thought. And so they remain unrepentant, for after all they have destroyed nothing. They no more desire a powerful king than an heroic liberator or religious authority. In all innocence they want the established order to continue, but they have the more or less certain reflective knowledge that it no longer exists. Then they proudly imagine that their attitude is ironical—as though real irony were not essentially a concealed enthusiasm in a negative age (just as the hero is enthusiasm made manifest in a positive age), as though irony did not involve sacrifice, when its greatest master was put to death.

This reflective tension ultimately constitutes itself into a principle, and just as in a passionate age *enthusiasm* is the unifying principle, so in an age which is very reflective and passionless *envy* is the negative unifying principle. This must not, however, be interpreted as an ethical charge; the idea of reflection is, if one may so express it, envy, and it is therefore twofold in its action: it is selfish within the individual and it results in the selfishness of the society around him, which thus works against him.

The envy in reflection (within the individual) prevents him making a decision passionately. If, for a moment, it should seem as though an individual were about to succeed in throwing off the yoke of reflection, he is at once pulled up by the opposition of the reflection which surrounds him. The envy which springs from reflection imprisons man's will and his strength. First of all the individual has to break loose from the bonds of his own reflection, but even then he is not free. Instead he finds himself in the vast prison formed by the reflection of those around him, for because of his relation to his own reflection he also has a certain relation to the reflection around him. He can only escape from this second imprisonment through the inwardness of religion, no matter how clearly he may perceive the falseness of the situation. With every means in its power reflection prevents people from realizing that both the individual and the age are thus imprisoned, not imprisoned by tyrants or priests or nobles or the secret police, but by reflection itself, and it does so by maintaining the flattering and conceited notion that the *possibility* of reflection is far superior to a mere *decision*. A selfish envy makes such demands upon the individual that by asking too much it prevents him from doing anything. It spoils him like an indulgent mother, for the envy within him prevents the individual from devoting himself to others. Moreover, the envy which surrounds him and in which he participates by envying others, is envious in a negative and critical sense.

But the further it is carried the more clearly does the envy of reflection become a moral *ressentiment*. Just as air in a sealed space becomes poisonous, so the imprisonment

of reflection develops a culpable *ressentiment* if it is not ven-
tilated by action or incident of any kind. In reflection the
state of strain (or tension as we called it) results in the neu-
tralization of all the higher powers, and all that is low and
despicable comes to the fore, its very impudence giving the
spurious effect of strength, while protected by its very base-
ness it avoids attracting the attention of *ressentiment*.

It is a fundamental truth of human nature that man is
incapable of remaining permanently on the heights, of con-
tinuing to admire anything. Human nature needs variety.
Even in the most enthusiastic ages people have always liked
to joke enviously about their superiors. That is perfectly
in order and is entirely justifiable so long as after having
laughed at the great they can once more look upon them with
admiration; otherwise the game is not worth the candle. In
that way *ressentiment* finds an outlet even in an enthusiastic
age. And as long as an age, even though less enthusiastic, has
the strength to give *ressentiment* its proper character and has
made up its mind what its expression signifies, *ressentiment*
has its own, though dangerous, importance. In Greece, for
example, the form *ressentiment* took was ostracism, a self-
defensive effort, as it were, on the part of the masses to pre-
serve their equilibrium in face of the outstanding qualities of
the eminent. The outstanding man was exiled, but every one
understood how dialectical the relationship was, ostracism
being a mark of distinction. Thus, in representing a some-
what earlier period in the spirit of Aristophanes, it would be

more ironical to let a completely unimportant person be ostracized than to let him become dictator, because ostracism is the negative mark of greatness. But it would be still better to let the story end with the people recalling the man whom they had ostracized because they could no longer do without him, and he would then be a complete mystery to the country of his exile, which would, of course, be quite unable to discover anything remarkable about him. In *The Knights* Aristophanes gives us a picture of the final state of corruption in which the vulgar rabble ends when—just as in Tibet they worship the Dalai Lama's excrement—they contemplate their own scum in its representatives; and that, in a democracy, is a degree of corruption comparable to auctioning the crown in a monarchy. But as long as *ressentiment* still has any character, ostracism is a negative mark of distinction. The man who told Aristides that he had voted for his exile 'because he could not endure hearing Aristides called the only just man' did not deny Aristides' eminence, but admitted something about himself. He admitted that his relation to distinction was the unhappy love of envy, instead of the happy love of admiration, but he did not try to belittle that distinction.

On the other side, the more reflection gets the upper hand and thus makes people indolent, the more dangerous *ressentiment* becomes, because it no longer has sufficient character to make it conscious of its significance. Bereft of that character reflection is cowardly and vacillating, and according to circumstances interprets the same thing in a variety of ways. It tries to treat it as a joke, and if that fails, to regard it as an insult, and when that fails, to dismiss it as nothing at all; or else it will treat the thing as a witticism, and if that fails then say that it was meant as a moral satire deserving attention, and if that does not succeed, add that it is not worth bothering about.

Thus *ressentiment* becomes the constituent principle of want of character, which from utter wretchedness tries to sneak itself a position, all the time safeguarding itself by conceding that it is less than nothing. The *ressentiment* which results from want of character can never understand that eminent distinction really is distinction. Neither does it understand itself by recognizing distinction negatively (as in the case of ostracism) but wants to drag it down, wants to belittle it so that it really ceases to be distinguished. And *ressentiment* not only defends itself against all *existing* forms of distinction but against that which is still *to come*.

The *ressentiment* which is *establishing itself* is the process of levelling, and while a passionate age storms ahead setting up new things and tearing down old, raising and demolishing as it goes, a reflective and passionless age does exactly the contrary: it *hinders and stifles* all action; it levels. Levelling is a silent, mathematical, and abstract occupation which shuns upheavals. In a burst of momentary enthusiasm people might, in their despondency, even long for a misfortune in order to feel the powers of life, but the apathy which follows is no more helped by a disturbance than an engineer levelling a piece of land. At its most violent a rebellion is like a volcanic eruption and drowns every other sound. At its maximum the levelling process is a deathly silence in which one can hear one's heart beat, a silence which nothing can pierce, in which everything is engulfed, powerless to resist. One man can be at the head of a rebellion, but no one can be at the head of the levelling process alone, for in that case he would be the leader and would thus escape being levelled. Each individual within his own little circle can co-operate in the levelling, but it is an abstract power, and the levelling process is the victory of abstraction over the individual. The levelling process in modern times, corresponds, in reflection, to fate in antiquity.

The dialectic of antiquity tended towards leadership (the great individual and the masses—the free man and the slaves); so far the dialectic of Christendom tends towards representation (the majority sees itself in its representative and is set free by the consciousness that it is the majority which it represented, in a sort of self-consciousness); the dialectic of the present age tends towards equality, and its most logical—though mistaken—fulfilment is levelling, as the negative unity of the negative reciprocity of all individuals.

It must be obvious to every one that the profound significance of the levelling process lies in the fact that it means the predominance of the category 'generation' over the category 'individuality'. In antiquity the total number of the individuals was there to express, as it were, the value of the outstanding individual. Nowadays the standard of value has been changed so that *equally,* approximately so and so many men go to one individual, and one need only be sure of having the right number in order to have importance. In antiquity the individual in the masses had no importance whatsoever; the outstanding individual signified them all. The present age tends towards a mathematical equality in which equally in all classes approximately so and so many people go to one individual. Formerly the outstanding individual could allow himself everything and the individual in the masses nothing at all. Now everyone knows that so and so many make an individual and quite consistently people add themselves together (it is called joining together, but that is only a polite euphemism) for the most trivial purposes. Simply in order to put a passing whim into practice a few people add themselves together, and the thing is done— then they dare do it. For that reason not even a preeminently gifted man can free himself from reflection, because he very soon becomes conscious of himself as a fractional part in some quite trivial matter, and so fails to achieve the infinite freedom of religion. The fact that several people united together have the courage to meet death does not nowadays mean that each, individually, has the courage, for, even more than death, the individual fears the judgement and protest of reflection upon his wishing to risk something on his own. The individual no longer belongs to God, to himself, to his beloved, to his art or to his science, he is conscious of belonging in all things to an abstraction to which he is subjected by reflection, just as a serf belongs to an estate. That is why people band together in cases where it is an absolute contradiction to be more than one. The apotheosis of the positive principle of association is nowadays the devouring and demoralizing principle which in the slavery of reflection makes even virtues into *vitia splendida*. There is no other reason for this than that eternal responsibility, and the religious singling out of the individual before God, is ignored. When corruption sets in at that point people seek consolation in company, and so reflection catches the individual for life. And those who do not realize even the beginning of this crisis are engulfed without further ado in the reflective relationship.

The levelling process is not the action of an individual but the work of reflection in the hands of an abstract power. It is therefore possible to calculate the law governing it in the same way that one calculates the diagonal in a parallelogram of forces. The individual who levels down is himself engulfed in the process and so on, and while he seems to know selfishly what he is doing one can only say of people *en masse* that they know not what they do; for just as collective enthusiasm produces a surplus which does not come from the individual, there is also a surplus in this case. A demon is called up over whom no individual has any power, and though the very abstraction of levelling gives the individual a momentary, selfish kind of enjoyment, he is at the same time signing the warrant for his own doom. Enthusiasm *may* end in disaster, but levelling is *eo ipso* the destruction of the individual. No age, and therefore not the present age, can bring the scepticism of that process to a halt, for as soon as it tries to stop it, the law of the levelling process is again called into action. It can therefore only be held up by the individual attaining the religious courage which springs from his individual religious isolation.

I was once the witness of a street fight in which three men most shamefully set upon a fourth. The crowd stood and watched them with indignation; expressions of disgust began to enliven the scene; then several of the onlookers set on one of the three assailants and knocked him down and beat him. The avengers had, in fact, applied precisely the same rules as the offenders. If I may be allowed to do so, I will introduce my own unimportant self into the story and continue. I went up to one of the avengers and tried by argument to explain to him how illogical his behaviour was; but it seemed quite impossible for him to discuss the question: he could only repeat that such a rascal richly deserved to have three people against him. The humour of the situation would have been even more apparent to some one who had not seen the beginning of the brawl, and so simply heard one man saying of another (who was alone) that he was three against one, and heard the remark just when the very reverse was the case—when they were three to one against him. In

the first place it was humorous because of the contradiction
which it involved, as when the policeman told a man standing in the street 'to kindly disperse'. Secondly it had all the
humour of self-contradiction. But what I learnt from it was
that I had better give up all hope of putting a stop to that
scepticism, lest it should turn upon me.

No single individual (I mean no outstanding individual—in the sense of leadership and conceived according
to the dialectical category 'fate') will be able to arrest the
abstract process of levelling, for it is negatively something
higher, and the age of chivalry is gone. No society or association can arrest that abstract power, simply because an
association is itself in the service of the levelling process.
Not even the individuality of the different nationalities can
arrest it, for on a higher plane the abstract process of levelling is a negative representation of *humanity pure and unal-
loyed*. The abstract levelling process, that self-combustion of
the human race, produced by the friction which arises when
the individual ceases to exist as singled out by religion, is
bound to continue, like a trade wind, and consume everything. But through it each individual for himself may receive
once more a religious education and, in the highest sense,
will be helped by the *examen rigorosum* of the levelling process to an essentially religious attitude. For the younger men
who, however strongly they personally may cling to what
they admire as eminent, realize from the beginning that the
levelling process is evil in both the selfish individual and in

the selfish generation, but that it can also, if they desire it honestly and before God, become the starting-point for the highest life—for them it will indeed be an education to live in the age of levelling. Their age will, in the very highest sense, develop them religiously and at the same time educate them aesthetically and intellectually, because in this way the comic will receive its absolute expression. The highest form of the comic arises precisely when the individual comes directly under the infinite abstraction of 'pure humanity,' without any of those intermediary qualifications which temper the humour of man's position and strengthen its pathos, without any of the concrete particulars of organization which the levelling process destroys. But that again is only another expression of the fact that man's only salvation lies in the reality of religion for each individual.

And it will add fuel to their enthusiasm to understand that it is in fact through error that the individual is given access to the highest, if he courageously desires it. But the levelling process will have to continue, and must be completed, just as the scandal had to come into the world, though woe to them by whom it comes.

It has often been said that a reformation should begin with each man reforming himself. That, however, is not what actually happened, for the reformation produced a hero who paid God dearly enough for his position as hero. By joining up with him directly people buy cheap, indeed at bargain prices, what he had paid for so dearly; but they do not buy the highest of all things. The abstract principle of levelling, on the contrary, like the biting east wind, has no personal relation to any individual but has only an abstract relationship which is the same for every one. There, no hero suffers for others, or helps them; the taskmaster of all alike is the levelling process which itself takes on their education. And the man who learns most from the levelling and himself becomes greatest does not become an outstanding man or a hero—that would only impede the levelling process, which is rigidly consistent to the end—he himself prevents that from happening because he has understood the meaning of levelling; he becomes a man and nothing else, in the complete equalitarian sense. That is the idea of religion. But, under those conditions, the equalitarian order is severe and the profit is seemingly very small; seemingly, for unless the individual learns in the reality of religion and before God to be content with himself, and learns, instead of dominating others, to dominate himself, content as priest to be his own audience, and as author his own reader, if he will not learn to be satisfied with that as the highest, because it is the expression of the equality of all men before God and of our likeness to others, then he will not escape from reflection. It may be that for one deceptive moment it will seem to him, in relation to his gifts, as though he were levelling, but in the end he will sink down beneath the levelling process. There is no good calling upon a Holger Danske or a Martin Luther; their day is over and at bottom it is only the individual's laziness which makes a man long to have them back, a worldly impatience which prefers to buy something cheap, second-hand, rather than to buy the highest of all things very dear and first-hand. It is worse than useless to found society after society, because negatively speaking there is something above them, even though the short-sighted member of the society cannot see it.

The principle of individuality in its *immediate* and beautiful formation is symbolized for the generation in the outstanding and eminent individual; it groups subordinate individualities round the representative. This principle of individuality, in its *eternal* truth, uses the abstraction and equality of the generation to level down, and in that way co-operates in developing the individual religiously into a real man. For the levelling process is as powerful where temporary things are concerned as it is impotent where eternal things are concerned. Reflection is a snare in which one is caught, but, once the 'leap' of enthusiasm has been taken, the relation is a different one and it becomes a noose which drags one into eternity. Reflection is and remains the hardest creditor in existence; hitherto it has cunningly bought up all the possible views of life, but it cannot buy the essentially religious and eternal view of life; on the other hand, it can tempt people astray with its dazzling brilliance, and dishearten them by reminding them of all the past. But, by leaping into the depths, one learns to help oneself, learns to love others as much as oneself, even though one is accused of

arrogance and pride—because one will not accept help—or
of selfishness, because one will not cunningly deceive people
by helping them, i.e. by helping them to escape their highest
destiny.

Should any one complain that what I have set forth here
is known to all and could be said by any one, then my answer
is: the more the merrier—I am not asking for a position of
eminence and I have nothing against every one knowing my
opinion, unless that were to mean, in a sense, that it is to be
taken from me and thereby put at the disposal of a negative
association. So long as I have permission to retain them, my
opinions do not lose their value by being known to every
one.

Throughout many changes the tendency in modern times
has remained a levelling one. These changes themselves have
not, however, all of them, been levelling, for they are none of
them abstract enough, each having a certain concrete reality. To some extent it is true that the levelling process goes
on when one great man attacks another, so that both are
weakened, or when one is neutralized by the other, or when
an association of people, in themselves weak, grow stronger than the eminent. Levelling can also be accomplished
by one particular caste, e.g. the clergy, the bourgeois, the
peasants, by the people themselves. But all that is only the
first movement of an abstract power within the concreteness
of individuality.

In order that everything should be reduced to the same level, it is first of all necessary to procure a phantom, its spirit, a monstrous abstraction, an all-embracing something which is nothing, a mirage—and that phantom is *the public.* It is only in an age which is without passion, yet reflective, that such a phantom can develop itself with the help of the Press which itself becomes an abstraction. In times of passion and tumult and enthusiasm, even when a people desire to realize a fruitless idea and lay waste and destroy everything: even then there is no such thing as a public. There are parties and they are concrete. The Press, in times such as those, takes on a concrete character according to the division of parties. But just as sedentary professional people are the first to take up any fantastic illusion which comes their way, so a passionless, sedentary, reflective age, in which only the Press exhibits a vague sort of life, fosters this phantom. The public is, in fact, the real Levelling-Master rather than the actual leveller, for whenever levelling is only approximately accomplished it is done by something, but the public is a monstrous nothing. The public is a concept which could not have occurred in antiquity because the people *en masse, in corpore,* took part in any situation which arose, and were responsible for the actions of the individual, and, moreover, the individual was personally present and had to submit at once to applause or disapproval for his decision. Only when the sense of association in society is no longer strong enough to give life to concrete realities is the Press able to create that abstraction 'the public', consisting of unreal individuals who never are and never can be united in an actual situation or organization—and yet are held together as a whole.

The public is a host, more numerous than all the peoples together, but it is a body which can never be reviewed, it cannot even be represented, because it is an abstraction. Nevertheless, when the age is reflective and passionless and destroys everything concrete, the public becomes everything and is supposed to include everything. And that again shows how the individual is thrown back upon himself.

The real moment in time and the real situation being simultaneous with real people, each of whom is something: that is what helps to sustain the individual. But the existence of a public produces neither a situation nor simultaneity. The individual reader of the Press is not the public, and even though little by little a number of individuals or even all of them should read it, the simultaneity is lacking. Years might be spent gathering the public together, and still it would not be there. This abstraction, which the individuals so illogically form, quite rightly repulses the individual instead of coming to his help. The man who has no opinion of an event at the actual moment accepts the opinion of the majority, or, if he is quarrelsome, of the minority. But it must be remembered that both majority and minority are real people, and that is why the individual is assisted by adhering to them. A public, on the contrary, is an abstraction. To adopt the opinion of this or that man means that one knows that they will be subjected to the same dangers as oneself, that they will be led astray with one if the opinion leads astray. But to adopt the same opinion as the public is a deceptive consolation because the public is only there *in abstracto*. Whilst, therefore, no majority has ever been so certain of being right and victorious as the public, that is not much consolation to the individual, for a public is a phantom which forbids all personal contact. And if a man adopts public opinion today and is hissed to-morrow he is hissed by the public.

A generation, a people, an assembly of the people, a meeting or a man, are responsible for what they are and can be made ashamed if they are inconstant and unfaithful; but a public remains a public. A people, an assembly or a man can change to such an extent that one may say: they are no longer the same; a public on the other hand can become the very opposite and still be the same—a public. But it is precisely by means of this abstraction and this abstract discipline that the individual will be formed (in so far as the individual is not already formed by his inner life), if he does not succumb in the process, taught to be content, in the highest religious sense, with himself and his relation to God, to be at one with himself instead of being in agreement with a public which destroys everything that is relative, concrete and particular in life; educated to find peace within himself and with God, instead of counting hands. And the ultimate difference between the modern world and antiquity is: that 'the whole' is not concrete and is therefore unable to support the individual, or to educate him as the concrete should (though without developing him absolutely), but is an abstraction which by its abstract equality repels him and thus helps him to be educated absolutely—unless he succumbs in the process. The *taedium vitae* so constant in antiquity was due to the fact that the outstanding individual was what others *could not be;* the inspiration of modern times will be that any man who finds himself, religiously speaking, has only achieved what *every one can achieve.*

A public is neither a nation, nor a generation, nor a community, nor a society, nor these particular men, for all these are only what they are through the concrete; no single person who belongs to the public makes a real commitment; for some hours of the day, perhaps, he belongs to the public—at moments when he is nothing else, since when he really is what he is he does not form part of the public. Made up of such individuals, of individuals at the moments when they are nothing, a public is a kind of gigantic something, an abstract and deserted void which is everything and nothing. But on this basis any one can arrogate to himself a public, and just as the Roman Church chimerically extended its frontiers by appointing bishops *in partibus infidelium,* so a public is something which every one can claim, and even a drunken sailor exhibiting a 'peep-show' has dialectically absolutely the same right to a public as the greatest man; he has just as logical a right to put all those many noughts *in front* of his single number.

A public is everything and nothing, the most dangerous of all powers and the most insignificant: one can speak to a whole nation in the name of the public, and still the public will be less than a single real man, however unimportant. The qualification 'public' is produced by the deceptive juggling of an age of reflection, which makes it appear flattering to the individual who in this way can arrogate to himself this monster, in comparison with which concrete realities seem poor. The public is the fairy story of an age of understanding, which in imagination makes the individual into something even greater than a king above his people*; but the public is also a gruesome abstraction through which the individual will receive his religious formation—or sink.

The Press is an abstraction (since a paper is not a concrete part of a nation and only in an abstract sense an individual) which in conjunction with the passionless and reflective character of the age produces that abstract phantom: a public which in its turn is really the levelling power. Consequently it has an importance apart from its negative religious importance.

The fewer ideas there are at any time, the more indolent

---

* As an author I have fortunately never sought for or had a public, but have contented myself with 'the individual', and on account of that limitation have almost become a proverb.

[All Kierkegaard's religious discourses, which form a large part of his works, were dedicated to " 'that individual', whom with joy and thankfulness I call my reader because he reads, not thinking of the author, but of God".]

and exhausted by bursts of enthusiasm will it be; nevertheless, if we imagine the Press growing weaker and weaker because no events or ideas catch hold of the age, the more easily will the process of levelling become a harmful pleasure, a form of sensual intoxication which flames up for a moment, simply making the evil worse and the conditions of salvation more difficult and the probability of decline more certain. Although the demoralization brought about by autocracy and the decay of revolutionary periods have often been described, the decay of an age without passion is something just as harmful, though, on account of its ambiguity, it is less obvious.

It may not be without interest to consider this point. More and more individuals, owing to their bloodless indolence, will aspire to be nothing at all—in order to become the public: that abstract whole formed in the most ludicrous way, by all participants becoming a third party (an onlooker). This indolent mass which understands nothing and does nothing itself, this gallery, is on the look-out for distraction and soon abandons itself to the idea that everything that any one does is done in order to give it (the public) something to gossip about. That indolent mass sits with its legs crossed, wearing an air of superiority, and anyone who tries to work, whether king, official, school-teacher or the better type of journalist, the poet or the artist, has to struggle to drag the public along with it, while the public thinks in its own superior way that it is the horse.

If I tried to imagine the public as a particular person (for although some better individuals momentarily belong to the public they nevertheless have something concrete about them, which holds them in its grip even if they have not attained the supreme religious attitude), I should perhaps think of one of the Roman emperors, a large well-fed figure, suffering from boredom, looking only for the sensual intoxication of laughter, since the divine gift of wit is not earthly enough. And so for a change he wanders about, indolent rather than bad, but with a negative desire to dominate. Every one who has read the classical authors knows how many things a Caesar could try out in order to kill time. In the same way the public keeps a dog to amuse it. That dog is the sum of the literary world.* If there is some one superior to the rest, perhaps even a great man, the dog is set on him and the fun begins. The dog goes for him, snapping and tearing at his coat-tails, allowing itself every possible ill-mannered familiarity—until the public tires, and says it may stop. That is an example of how the public levels. Their betters and superiors in strength are mishandled—and the dog remains a dog which even the public despises. The levelling is therefore done by a third party; a nonexistent public levelling with the help of a third party which in its insignificance is less than nothing, being already more than levelled. And so the public is unrepentant, for it was after all not the

---

* *The Corsair,* the paper in which Kierkegaard was lampooned.

public that acted but the dog; just as one says to children—
the cat's mother did it. The public is unrepentant—it was not
really belittling any one; it just wanted a little amusement.
For had the levelling implement been remarkably energetic,
the indolent public would have been fooled because the implement itself would have been in the way; but when their
betters are held down by the insignificant and the insignificant by itself, then no one is quit of anything.

The public is unrepentant, for it is not they who own the
dog—they only subscribe. They neither set the dog on any
one, nor whistle it off—directly. If asked they would answer:
the dog is not mine, it has no master. And if the dog had to
be killed they would say: it was really a good thing that bad-
tempered dog was put down, every one wanted it killed—
even the subscribers.

Perhaps some one, familiarizing himself with such a case,
and inclined to fix his attention upon the outstanding individual who suffered at the hands of the public, may be of the
opinion that such an ordeal is a great misfortune. I cannot
at all agree with such an opinion, for any one who really
wishes to be helped to attain the highest is in fact benefited
by undergoing such a misfortune, and must rather desire it
even though people may be led to rebel. The really terrible
thing is the thought of all the lives that are or easily may be
wasted. I will not even mention those who are lost, or at any
rate led completely astray: those who play the part of the dog
for money, but the many who are helpless, thoughtless and

sensual, who live superior lazy lives and never receive any deeper impression of existence than this meaningless grin, and all those bad people who are led into further temptation because in their stupidity they even become self-important by commiserating with the one who is attacked, without even understanding that in such a position the person attacked is always the stronger, without understanding that in this case the terrible and ironical truth applies: Weep not over him but over yourselves.

That is the levelling process at its lowest, for it always equates itself to the divisor by means of which every one is reduced to a common denominator. Eternal life is also a sort of levelling, and yet that is not so, because the common denominator is that every one should really and essentially be a man in in a religious sense.

Hitherto I have been dealing with the dialectical categories and qualifications, and with their consequences, whether actually present at any given moment or not. I shall now abandon the dialectical analysis of the present age in order to arrive dialectically at its concrete affirmations regarding everyday life. It is here that the darker side will be seen; but although this cannot be denied, it is equally certain that just as reflection itself is not evil, so a very reflective age has its lighter side, simply because a higher degree of reflection implies greater significance than immediate passion; for when enthusiasm intervenes to gather the powers of reflection together into a decision, and because reflection confers, on the average, a greater capacity for action—then, when religion enters in, it takes command of that increased capacity for action.

Reflection is not the evil; but a reflective condition and the deadlock which it involves, by transforming the capacity for action into a means of escape from action, is both corrupt and dangerous, and leads in the end to a retrograde movement.

The present age is essentially one of understanding lacking in passion, and has therefore abolished the *principle of contradiction*. By comparison with a passionate age, an age without passion gains in *scope what it loses in intensity*. But this scope may once again become the condition of a still higher form, if a corresponding intensity assumes control of the extended field of activity which is put at its disposal. The abolition of the principle of contradiction, expressed in terms of existence, means to live in contradiction with oneself. The creative omnipotence of the differentiating power of passion, which makes the individual completely at one with himself, is transformed into the extended scope of reflective understanding: as a result of knowing and being everything possible, one is in contradiction with oneself, i.e. nothing at all. The principle of contradiction strengthens the individual's faithfulness to himself and makes him as constant as the number three spoken of so beautifully by Socrates, when he says that it would rather endure anything than become four or even a large round number, and in the same way the individual would rather suffer and be true to himself than be all manner of things in contradiction with himself.

What is *talkativeness*? It is the result of doing away with the vital distinction between talking and keeping silent. Only some one who knows how to remain essentially silent can really talk—and act essentially. Silence is the essence of inwardness, of the inner life. Mere gossip anticipates real talk, and to express what is still in thought weakens action by forestalling it. But some one who can really talk, because he knows how to remain silent, will not talk about a variety of things but about one thing only, and he will know when to talk and when to remain silent. Where mere scope is concerned, talkativeness wins the day, it jabbers on incessantly about everything and nothing. When people's attention is no longer turned inwards, when they are no longer satisfied with their own inner religious lives, but turn to others and to things outside themselves, where the relation is intellectual, in search of that satisfaction, when nothing important ever happens to gather the threads of life together with the finality of a catastrophe: that is the time for talkativeness. In a passionate age great events (for they correspond to each other) give people something to talk about. Talkativeness, on the contrary, has, in quite another sense, plenty to talk about. And when the event is over, and silence follows, there is still something to remember and to think about while one remains silent. But talkativeness is afraid of the silence which reveals its emptiness.

The law governing artistic production applies, on a smaller scale, to every one in daily life. Every man who has a real experience experiences at the same time all its possibilities in an ideal sense, including the opposite possibility. Aesthetically these possibilities are his lawful property. Not so, however, his private and personal reality. His talk and his production both rest upon his silence. The ideal perfection of his talk and of his production will correspond to his silence, and the absolute expression of that silence will be that the ideal will include the qualitatively opposite possibility. But as soon as the artist prostitutes his own reality he is no longer essentially productive. His beginning is his end, and his very first word will be a sin against the modesty of the ideal. This type of artistic production is therefore even, aesthetically speaking, a kind of private gossip. It is easily recognized because it is not balanced by its opposite; for ideality is the balance of opposites. For example, if the man who is moved to write by suffering is really initiated into the realm of ideals, he will reproduce the happiness as well as the suffering of his experience with the same affection. The condition of his attaining this ideal is the silence with which he shuts off his own real personality. Otherwise, in spite of all precautions, such as changing the scene to Africa, his one-sided predilection will be privately recognizable. For an author, like any one else, must have his own private personality, but it must be his own ἄδυτον[*]; and just as the entrance to a house is barred by the crossed bayonets of the guards, the approach to a man's personality is barred by the dialectical cross of qualitative opposites in an ideal equilibrium.

What is true of the greater relationship and is very clear in the above circumstances, which is why they were instanced, is also true in a lesser degree of the smaller ones; and, once again, silence is the *conditio sine qua non* of all educated social intercourse. The more thoroughly a man grasps the ideal and the idea—in silence—the more capable will he be of reproducing man's daily life so that it seems as though he only talked of particular things at a certain distance. The less ideal, the more superficial his talk, and his conversation will become a meaningless repetition of names, of 'absolutely reliable' private information of what this and that person—mentioning all their names—had said, &c. &c., and conversation in general will take on a talkative confidential note about what one is doing or going to do, what one would have said on a certain occasion, which particular girl one is making love to, why nevertheless one does not want to marry. The introspection of silence is the condition of all educated social intercourse; the exteriorized caricature of inwardness is vulgarity and talkativeness.

---

* Holy of Holies.

One finds excellent examples of the kind of talkativeness I am referring to in the novel.* It consists entirely of trivialities, people's names are always mentioned and they are people whose trivial way of life is interesting because of their names. People who are talkative certainly chatter away about something and, indeed, their one wish is to have an excuse for more gossip, but the subject is non-existent from the ideal point of view. It always consists of some trivial fact such as that Mr. Marsden is engaged and has given his fiancée a Persian shawl; that Petersen, the poet, is going to write some new poems, or that Marcussen, the actor, mispronounced a certain word last night. If we could suppose for a moment that there was a law which did not forbid people talking, but simply ordered that everything which was spoken about should be treated as though it had happened fifty years ago, the gossips would be done for, they would be in despair. On the other hand, it would not really interfere with any one who could really talk. That an actor should have mispronounced a word could only be interesting if there was something interesting in the mispronunciation itself, in which case the fifty years make no difference—but Miss Gusta, for example, would be in despair, she who had been at the theatre that very evening, in a box with Alderman Waller's wife; for was it not *she* who noticed the slip and even noticed a member of the chorus smiling, &c. &c. It

---

* Which Kierkegaard was reviewing: *The Two Ages*.

really would be a shame and cruelty to all those silly gossiping people who must all the same be allowed to live—and so the law is only posited.

With gossip, therefore, the vital distinction between what is private and what is public is obliterated, and everything is reduced to a kind of private-public gossip which corresponds more or less to the public of which it forms part. The public is public opinion which interests itself in the most private concerns. Something that nobody would dare to tell to a gathering, that nobody could *talk* about, and which even the gossips would not like to admit to having gossiped about, can perfectly well be written for the public and, as a member of the public, people may know all about it.

What is *formlessness?* It is the result of doing away with the vital distinction between form and content. Formlessness may, therefore, unlike madness or stupidity, have a content that is true, but the truth it contains can never be essentially true. It will be capable of being extended so as to include everything or touch upon everything, whereas a real content is clearly, and, if one likes, miserably limited because of its intensity and self-absorption.

The universality of formlessness in a passionless but reflective age is expressed, moreover, not only by the fact that the most varied ideas are found dallying in the same company but by the diametrically opposite fact that people find a paramount longing for and pleasure in 'acting on principle'. A principle, as the word indicates, is what comes first, i.e. the substance, the idea in the undeveloped form of feeling and of enthusiasm which drives on the individual by its own inner power. That is entirely wanting in a passionless individual. To him a principle is something purely external for the sake of which he does one thing as willingly as another, and the opposite of both into the bargain. The life of an individual without passion is not the development of a self-revealing principle. On the contrary, his inner life is something hurrying along, always on the move and always hurrying to do something 'on principle'. A principle, in that sense, becomes a monstrous something or other, an abstraction, just like the public. And while the public is something or other so monstrous that not all the nations of the world and all the souls in eternity put together are as numerous, every one, even a drunken sailor, can have a public, and the same is true of 'a principle'. It is something immense which even the most insignificant man can add to the most insignificant action, and thus become tremendously self-important. When an honest insignificant man suddenly becomes a hero for the sake of a principle, the result is quite as comic as though fashion decreed that every one was to wear a cap with a peak thirty feet long. If a man had a little button sewn on the inner pocket of his coat 'on principle' his otherwise unimportant and quite serviceable action would become charged with importance—it is not improbable that it would result in the formation of a society.

It is acting 'on principle' which does away with the vital distinction which constitutes decency. For decency is immediate (whether the immediateness is original or acquired). It has its seat in feeling and in the impulse and consistency of an inner enthusiasm. 'On principle' one can do anything and what one does is, fundamentally, a matter of indifference, just as a man's life remains insignificant even though 'on principle' he gives his support to all the 'needs of the times', even when, by virtue of being a mute and in that capacity as 'the organ of public opinion' he is as well known as the figures on a barrel-organ that can move forward and bow, plate in hand. 'On principle' a man can do anything, take part in anything and himself remain inhuman and indeterminate. 'On principle' a man may interest himself in the founding of a brothel (there are plenty of social studies on the subject written by the health authorities), and the same man can 'on principle' assist in the publication of a new Hymn Book because it is supposed to be the great need of the times. But it would be as unjustifiable to conclude from the first fact that he was debauched as it would, perhaps, be to conclude from the second that he read or sang hymns. In this way everything becomes permissible if done 'on principle'. The police can go to certain places on 'official duty' to which no one else can go, but as a result one cannot deduce anything from their presence. In the same way one can do anything 'on principle' and avoid all personal responsibility. People pull to pieces 'on principle' what they admire personally, which is nonsensical, for while it is true that everything creative is latently polemical, since it has to make room for the new which it is bringing into the world, a purely destructive process is nothing and its principle is emptiness—so what does it need space for? But modesty, repentance and responsibility cannot easily strike root in ground where everything is done, 'on principle'.

What is *superficiality* and the desire to show off? Superficiality is the result of doing away with the vital distinction between concealment and manifestation. It is the manifestation of emptiness, but where mere scope is concerned it wins, because it has the advantage of dazzling people with its brilliant shams. Real manifestation is homogeneous, because it is really profound, whereas superficiality has a varied and *omnium gatherum* appearance. Its love of showing off is the self-admiration of conceit in reflection. The concealment and reserve of inwardness is not given time in which to conceive an essential mystery, which can then be made manifest, but is disturbed long before that time comes and so, as a reward, reflection attracts the gaze of egotism upon its varied shams whenever possible.

What is *flirtation*? It is the result of doing away with the vital distinction between real love and real debauchery. Neither the real lover nor the real debauchee are guilty of flirting. A flirtation only toys with the possibility and is therefore a form of indulgence which dares to touch evil and fails to realize the good. To act 'on principle' is also a kind of flirtation, because it reduces moral action to an abstraction. But in mere scope flirtation has all the advantages, for one can flirt with anything, but one can only really love *one* girl. From the point of view of love, properly understood, any addition is really a subtraction (even though in a confused age a capricious man may be blinded by pleasure), and the more one adds the more one takes away.

What is *reasoning?* It is the result of doing away with the vital distinction which separates subjectivity and objectivity. As a form of abstract thought reasoning is not profoundly dialectical enough; as an opinion and a conviction it lacks full-blooded individuality. But where mere scope is concerned, reasoning has all the apparent advantage; for a thinker can encompass his science, a man can have an opinion upon a particular subject and a conviction as a result of a certain view of life, but one can reason about anything.

In our own day anonymity has acquired a far more pregnant significance than is perhaps realized: it has an almost epigrammatic significance. People not only write anonymously, they sign their anonymous works: they even talk anonymously. The very soul of a writer should go into his style, and a man puts his whole personality into the style of his conversation, though limited by the exception which Matthias Claudius noted when he said that if any one conjured a book its *esprit* should appear—unless there was no *esprit* in it. Nowadays one can talk with any one, and it must be admitted that people's opinions are exceedingly sensible, yet the conversation leaves one with the impression of having talked to an anonymity. The same person will say the most contradictory things and, with the utmost calm, make a remark, which coming from him is a bitter satire on his own life. The remark itself may be sensible enough, and of the kind that sounds well at a meeting, and may serve in a discussion preliminary to coming to a decision, in much the same way that paper is made out of rags. But all these opinions put together do not make one human, personal opinion such as you may hear from quite a simple man who talks about very little but really does talk. People's remarks are so objective, so all-inclusive, that it is a matter of complete indifference who expresses them, and where human speech is concerned that is the same as acting 'on principle'. And so our talk becomes like the public, a pure abstraction. There is no longer any one who knows how to talk, and instead, objective thought produces an atmosphere, an abstract sound, which makes human speech superfluous, just as machinery makes man superfluous. In Germany they even have phrasebooks for the use of lovers, and it will end with lovers sitting together talking anonymously. In fact there are handbooks for everything, and very soon education, all the world over, will consist in learning a greater or lesser number of comments by heart, and people will excel according to their capacity for singling out the various facts like a printer singling out the letters, but completely ignorant of the meaning of anything.

Thus our own age is essentially one of understanding, and on the average, perhaps, more knowledgeable than any former generation, but it is without passion. Every one knows a great deal, we all know which way we ought to go and all the different ways we can go, but nobody is willing to move. If at last some one were to overcome the reflection within him and happened to act, then immediately thousands of reflections would form an outward obstacle. Only a proposal to reconsider a plan is greeted with enthusiasm; action is met by indolence. Some of the superior and self-satisfied find the enthusiasm of the man who tried to act ridiculous, others are envious because he made a beginning when, after all, they *knew* just as well as he did what should be done—but did not do it. Still others use the fact that some one has acted in order to produce numerous critical observations and give vent to a store of arguments, demonstrating how much more sensibly the thing could have been done; others again, busy themselves guessing the outcome and, if possible, influencing events a little so as to favour their own hypothesis.

It is said that two English noblemen were once riding along a road when they met a man whose horse had run away with him and who, being in danger of falling off, shouted for help. One of the Englishmen turned to the other and said, 'A hundred guineas he falls off.' 'Taken,' said the other. With that they spurred their horses to a gallop and hurried on ahead to open the toll-gates and to prevent anything from getting in the way of the runaway horse. In the same way, though without that heroic and millionaire-like spleen, our own reflective and sensible age is like a curious, critical and worldly-wise person who, at the most, has vitality enough to lay a wager.

Life's existential tasks have lost the interest of reality; illusion cannot build a sanctuary for the divine growth of inwardness which ripens to decisions. One man is curious about another, every one is undecided, and their way of escape is to say that some one must come who will do something—and then they will bet on him.

It is quite impossible for the community or the idea of association to save our age. On the contrary, association is the scepticism, which is necessary in order that the development of individuality may proceed uniformly, so that the individual will either be lost or, disciplined by such abstractions, will find himself religiously. Nowadays the principle of association (which at the most is only valid where material interests are concerned) is not positive but negative; it is an escape, a distraction and an illusion. Dialectically the position is this: the principle of association, by strengthening the individual, enervates him; it strengthens numerically, but ethically that is a weakening. It is only after the individual has acquired an ethical outlook, in face of the whole world, that there can be any suggestion of really joining together. Otherwise the association of individuals who are in themselves weak, is just as disgusting and as harmful as the marriage of children.

Formerly the sovereign and the great each had their opinion and the rest were satisfied and decided enough to realize that they dared not or could not have an opinion. Now every one can have an opinion; but they have to band together numerically in order to have one. Twenty-five signatures make the most frightful stupidity into an opinion, and the considered opinion of a first-class mind is only a paradox. But when the context is meaningless it is useless to take a broad survey. The best that can be done is to consider each part of speech by itself. And if only nonsense comes out of a man's mouth it is useless to try and make a coherent speech, and it is better to take each word separately—and so with individuals.

The change which will come about is this. In the old order (which sprang from the relation between the individual and the generation) the officers, generals, heroes (i.e. the man of distinction, the leader within his own sphere) were *recognizable,* and every one (in proportion to his authority), with his little detachment, fitted picturesquely and organically into the whole, both supporting and supported by the whole. From now on the great man, the leader (according to his position) will be without authority because he will have divinely understood the diabolical principle of the levelling process; he will be *unrecognizable;* he will keep his distinction hidden like a plain-clothes policeman, and his support will only be negative, i.e. repelling people, whereas the infinite indifference of abstraction judges every individual and examines him in his isolation. This order is dialectically the very opposite of that of the Prophets and Judges, and just as the danger for them lay in their authority not being recognized so nowadays the unrecognizable is in danger of being recognized, and of being persuaded to accept recognition and importance as an authority, which could only hinder the highest development. For they are unrecognizable and go about their work like secret agents, not because of any private instruction from God!—for that is the case of Prophets and Judges—but are unrecognizable (without authority) because they have understood the universal in equality before God, and, because they realize this and their own responsibility every moment, are thus prevented from being guilty of thoughtlessly realizing in an inconsistent form this consistent perception. This order is dialectically the opposite of the organizing order symbolized in the outstanding personality, which makes the generation into a support for the individual, whereas now, like an abstraction, the generation is negatively supported by the unrecognizable, and turns polemically against the individual—in order to save every single individual religiously.

And so when the generation, which itself desired to level and to be emancipated, to destroy authority and at the same time itself, has, through the scepticism of the principle association, started the hopeless forest fire of abstraction; when as a result of levelling with this scepticism, the generation has rid itself of the individual and of everything organic and concrete, and put in its place 'humanity' and the numerical equality of man and man: when the generation has, for a moment, delighted in this unlimited panorama of abstract infinity, unrelieved by even the smallest eminence, undisturbed by even the slightest interest, a sea of desert; then the time has come for work to begin, for every individual must work for himself, each for himself. No longer can the individual, as in former times, turn to the great for help when he grows confused. That is past; he is either lost in the dizziness of unending abstraction or saved for ever in the reality of religion. Perhaps very many will cry out in despair, but it will not help them—already it is too late. If it is true that in former times authorities and powers were misused and brought upon themselves the nemesis of revolution, it was weakness and impotence which, desiring to stand alone, brought this final nemesis upon them. Nor shall any of the unrecognizable presume to help directly or to speak directly or to teach directly at the head of the masses, in order to direct their decisions, instead of giving his negative support and so helping the individual to make the decision which he himself has reached; any other course would be the end of him, because he would be indulging in the short-sighted compassion of man, instead of obeying the order of divinity, of an angry, yet so merciful, divinity. For the development is, in spite of everything, a progress because all the individuals who are saved will receive the specific weight of religion, its essence at first hand, from God himself. Then it will be said: 'behold, all is in readiness, see

how the cruelty of abstraction makes the true form of worldli-
ness only too evident, the abyss of eternity opens before you,
the sharp scythe of the leveller makes it possible for every one
individually to leap over the blade—and behold, it is God who
waits. Leap, then, into the arms of God'. But the 'unrecognizable' neither can nor dares help man, not even his most faithful disciple, his mother, or the girl for whom he would gladly
give his life: they must make the leap themselves, for God's
love is not a second-hand gift. And yet the 'unrecognizable'
(according to his degree) will have a double work compared
with the 'outstanding' man (of the same degree), because he
will not only have to work continuously, but at the same time
labour to conceal his work.

But the desolate abstraction of the levelling process will
always be continued by its servants, lest it should end with
a return of the old order. The servants of the levelling process are the servants of the powers of evil, for levelling itself
does not come from divinity and all good men will at times
grieve over its desolation, but divinity allows it and desires to
bring the highest into relation with the individual, i.e. with
each and every man. The servants of the levelling process are
known to him who is 'unrecognizable', but he dare not use
either power or authority against them, for that would be to
reverse the development, since it would become immediately
apparent to a third person that the 'unrecognizable' was an
authority, and in that way the third man would be prevented
from attaining to the highest.

Only by suffering can the 'unrecognizable' dare to help on the levelling process and, by the same suffering action, judge the instruments. He dare not overcome the levelling process directly, that would be his end, for it would be the same as acting with authority. But he will overcome it in suffering, and in that way express once more the law of his existence, which is not to dominate, to guide, to lead, but to serve in suffering and help indirectly. Those who have not made the leap will look upon his unrecognizable action, his suffering as failure; those who have made the leap will suspect that it was victory, but they can have no certainty, for they could only be made certain by him, and if he gave that certainty to a single person it would be the end of him, because he would have been unfaithful to the divinity in desiring to play at being authority: that would mean that he had failed; not only by being unfaithful to God in trying to use authority, but because he did not obey God and teach men to love one another by compelling himself, so that even though they begged him to do so he should not have deceived them by exerting authority.

But I break off. All this is only fooling, for if it is true that every man must work for his own salvation, then all the prophecies about the future of the world are only valuable and allowable as a recreation, or a joke, like playing bowls or cards.

But it must always be remembered that reflection is not in itself something harmful, that, on the contrary, it is nec-

essary to work through it in order that one's actions should
be more intensive. The stages of all actions which are performed with enthusiasm are as follows: first of all comes
immediate enthusiasm, then follows the stage of cleverness
which, because immediate enthusiasm does not calculate,
assumes with a calculating cleverness the appearance of
being the higher; and finally comes the highest and most
intensive enthusiasm which follows the stage of cleverness,
and is therefore able to see the shrewdest plan of action but
disdain it, and thereby receive the intensity of an eternal
enthusiasm. For the time being, however, and for some time
to come, this really intensive enthusiasm will remain completely misunderstood, and the question is whether it can
ever become popular, i.e. whether one may presume upon
such a degree of cleverness in the average man that cleverness will no longer seduce and enchant him, and may presume that he will be able to dominate it by having attained
the highest form of enthusiasm, but as it were squander
it—for an enthusiastic action, being always the opposite of
shrewd, is never obvious. The enthusiasm of Socrates was
not immediate. On the contrary, he was clever enough to
see what he had to do in order to escape, although he dis-
dained to act according to that opinion, just as he refused
the proffered speech. That is why there is nothing obvious
about his heroic death, and even in death he remained ironical by putting to the shrewd and the clever the question
whether he could really have been clever, since he did the

reverse. That is the point at which cleverness is left hanging in mid-air, hoisted with its own reflective judgement and that of the world about it, afraid that an action performed in the teeth of cleverness may be confused with an action performed without cleverness. An immediate enthusiasm does not know such a danger, and therefore requires the *impetus* of the most intense enthusiasm in order to get through life. Such an enthusiasm is not mere rhetorical twaddle about 'high seriousness', a still 'higher seriousness' and an 'all highest seriousness'. It can be known from its category: that it acts against understanding. Neither does immediate goodness know the danger of reflection—where goodness and weakness are mistaken and confused; and it is precisely for that reason that, after reflection, it requires a religious *impetus* to set goodness afloat again.

In our times, when so little is done, an extraordinary number of prophecies, apocalypses, glances at and studies of the future appear, and there is nothing to do but to join in and be one with the rest. Yet I have the advantage over the many who bear a heavy responsibility when they prophesy and give warnings, because I can be perfectly certain that no one would think of believing me. So I do not ask that any one should make a cross in their calendar or otherwise bother to see whether my words are fulfilled. If they are fulfilled, then people will have something else to think about than my accidental being and if they are not fulfilled, well, then I shall simply be a prophet in the modern sense of the word—for a prophet nowadays means to prognosticate and nothing more. In a certain sense a prophet cannot do anything else. It was providence that fulfilled the words of the older prophets, so perhaps we modern prophets, lacking the addition coming from providence, might say with Thales: what we predict will either happen or not; for to us too has God granted the gift of prophecy.

Of the Difference Between
a Genius and an Apostle

1847

What, exactly, have the errors[*] of exegesis and philosophy done in order to confuse Christianity, and how have they confused Christianity? Quite briefly and categorically, they have simply forced back the sphere of paradox-religion[†] into the sphere of aesthetics, and in consequence have succeeded in bringing Christian terminology to such a pass that terms which, so long as they remain within their sphere, are qualitative categories, can be put to almost any use as clever expressions. If the sphere of paradox-religion is abolished, or explained away in aesthetics, an Apostle becomes neither more nor less than a genius, and then—good night, Christianity! *Esprit* and the Spirit, revelation and originality, a call from God and genius, all end by meaning more or less the same thing.

---

[*] The errors, moreover, are not confined to heterodoxy but are also found in hyper-orthodoxy. They are in fact those of thoughtlessness.
[†] i.e. Christianity.

That is how the errors of science* and learning have confused Christianity. The confusion has spread from learning to the religious discourse, with the result that one not infrequently hears priests, *bona fide,* in all learned simplicity, prostituting Christianity. They talk in exalted terms of St. Paul's brilliance and profundity, of his beautiful similes and so on—that is mere aestheticism. If St. Paul is to be regarded as a genius, then things look black for him, and only clerical ignorance would ever dream of praising him in terms of aesthetics, because it has no standard, but argues that all is well so long as one says something good about him. This kind of good-natured and well-intentioned thoughtlessness is due to the fact that the individual in question is not disciplined by qualitative dialectic. If he were he would have learnt that to say something good of an Apostle, when it is inapposite, does him no service, for as a result he is acclaimed for what in this case is a matter of indifference, and admired as something which essentially he is not, and then what he is is quite forgotten. This kind of thoughtless eloquence is quite as likely to celebrate St. Paul as a stylist and an artist in words or, better still, since it is after all well known that he was also engaged in a craft, as a tent-maker whose masterly work surpassed that of all up-

---

* S. K. does not mean the natural sciences. The word used is the same as the German *Wissenschaft,* which means science as a method. Occasionally ? used learning.

holsterers before and since—for as long as one says something good about St. Paul all is well. As a genius St. Paul cannot be compared with either Plato or Shakespeare, as a coiner of beautiful similes he comes pretty low down in the scale, as a stylist his name is quite obscure—and as an upholsterer: well, I frankly admit I have no idea how to place him. The point is that it is always better to treat stupid solemnity as a joke and then the really serious thing becomes apparent, the fact that St. Paul is an Apostle. As an Apostle St. Paul has no connexion whatsoever with Plato or Shakespeare, with stylists or upholsterers, and none of them (Plato no more than Shakespeare or Harrison the upholsterer) can possibly be compared with him.

A genius and an Apostle are qualitatively different, they are definitions which each belong in their own spheres: *the sphere of immanence, and the sphere of transcendence:*

(I) *Genius may, therefore, have something new to bring forth, but what it brings forth disappears again as it becomes assimilated by the human race, just as the difference 'genius' disappears as soon as one thinks of eternity; the Apostle has, paradoxically, something new to bring, the newness of which, precisely because it is essentially paradoxical, and not an anticipation in relation to the development of the race, always remains, just as an Apostle remains an Apostle in all eternity, and no eternal immanence puts him on the same level as other men, because he is essentially, paradoxically different. (2) Genius is what it is of itself, i.e. through that which it is in itself; an Apostle is what he is by*

*his divine authority. (3) Genius has only an immanent teleology;
the Apostle is placed as absolute paradoxical teleology.*

All thought breathes in immanence, whereas faith and
the paradox are a qualitative sphere unto themselves. As
between man and man, *qua* man, all differences are immanent, vanishing before essential and eternal thought, a
factor which is certainly valid for the moment, but disappears in the essential equality of eternity. Genius is, as the
word itself shows, immediateness *(ingenium,* that which is
inborn, primitive, *primus,* original, *origo,* &c.),* it is a natural
qualification, genius *is born.* Even long before there can be
any question as to how far genius is prepared to relate its
particular gifts to God, it is genius, and it remains genius
even if it does not do so. It is possible that genius may so
change that it develops into what it is κάτα δύναμιν, so
as to acquire conscious possession of itself. If one uses the
expression 'paradox' in order to denote the something new
which a genius may have to bring forth, it is only used in an
inessential sense of the transitory paradox of the anticipation thus condensed into a paradox which, however, disappears again later. In his first communication a genius may

---

* *Genius* comes from the Latin *genius,* guardian spirit; but the word de-
rives from the stem of the verb *gigno,* to give birth, and seems originally
to have meant inherited power personified. Related to *genius* and *gigno*
is *ingenium,* gift (from *in-gigno,* that is to say 'in-born'). S. K. is therefore
right etymologically, though he did not know the root meaning of genius.
(Note in the Danish edition S.V. XI, edited by A. B. Drachmann.)

be paradoxical, but the more he comes to himself, the more completely will the paradox disappear. A genius may be a century ahead of his time, and therefore appear to be a paradox, but ultimately the race will assimilate what was once a paradox in such a way that it is no longer paradoxical.

It is otherwise with an Apostle. The word itself indicates the difference. An Apostle is not born; an Apostle is a man called and appointed by God, receiving a mission from him. An Apostle does not develop in such a way that he successively becomes what he is κάτα δύναμιν. For to become an Apostle is not preceded by any potential possibility; essentially every man is equally near to becoming one. An Apostle can never come to himself in such a way that he becomes conscious of his apostolic calling as a factor in the development of his life. Apostolic calling is a paradoxical factor, which from first to last in his life stands paradoxically outside his personal identity with himself as the definite person he is. A man may perhaps have reached years of discretion long ago, when suddenly he is called to be an Apostle. As a result of this call he does not become more intelligent, does not receive more imagination, a greater acuteness of mind and so on; on the contrary, he remains himself and by that paradoxical fact he is sent on a particular mission by God. By this paradoxical fact the Apostle is made paradoxically different from all other men for all eternity. The new which he may have to bring forth is the essential paradox. However long it may be proclaimed in the world it remains essentially and equally new, equally paradoxical, and no immanence can assimilate it. The Apostle did not behave like the man marked out by natural gifts who is born before his time; he was perhaps what we call a simple man, but by a paradoxical fact he was called to proclaim this new thing. Even if thought were to think that it could assimilate the doctrine, it cannot assimilate the way in which the doctrine came into the world; for the essential paradox is the protest against immanence. But the way in which a doctrine of this kind came into the world is qualitatively decisive, and it can only be ignored by deceit or by thoughtlessness.

(2) Genius is appreciated purely aesthetically, according to the measure of its content, and its specific weight; an Apostle is what he is through having divine authority. *Divine authority is, qualitatively, the decisive factor.* It is not by evaluating the content of the doctrine aesthetically or intellectually that I should or could reach the result: *ergo,* the man who proclaimed the doctrine was called by a revelation; *ergo,* he is an Apostle. The very reverse is the case: the man who is called by a revelation and to whom a doctrine is entrusted, argues from the fact that it is a revelation, from his authority. I have not got to listen to St. Paul because he is clever, or even brilliantly clever; I am to bow before St. Paul because he has divine authority; and in any case it remains St. Paul's responsibility to see that he produces that impression, whether anybody bows before his authority or not. St. Paul must not appeal to his cleverness, for in that case he is a fool;

he must not enter into a purely aesthetic or philosophical discussion of the content of the doctrine, for in that case he is side-tracked. No, he must appeal to his divine authority and, while willing to lay down his life and everything, by that very means *prevent* any aesthetic impertinence and any direct philosophic approach to the form and content of the doctrine. St. Paul has not to recommend himself and his doctrine with the help of beautiful similes; on the contrary, he should say to the individual: 'Whether the comparison is beautiful or whether it is worn and threadbare is all one, you must realize that what I say was entrusted to me by a revelation, so that it is God Himself or the Lord Jesus Christ who speaks, and you must not presumptuously set about criticizing the form. I cannot and dare not compel you to obey, but through your relation to God in your conscience I make you eternally responsible to God, eternally responsible for your relation to this doctrine, by having proclaimed it as revealed to me, and consequently proclaimed it with divine authority.'

Authority is the decisive quality. Or is there perhaps no difference, even within the relativity of human existence, and even though it disappears in immanence, between the king's command and the word of a poet or a thinker? And what is that difference if not that the king's command has authority and prohibits all aesthetic and critical impertinence as to the form and the content? But neither the poet nor the thinker has authority, even within his awn sphere of relativity; their statements are judged on purely aesthetic and philosophic grounds according to the value of the form and the content. The cause of the fundamental confusion in Christianity is surely that as a result of scepticism people are uncertain whether there is a God, and furthermore, that rebelling against all authorities they forget the meaning and dialectic of authority. A king is present physically and one can physically assure oneself of the fact, and should it become necessary he can give one decided physical proof that he is there. But God is not present in that sense. Scepticism has used this fact in order to put God on the same level as all those who have no authority, on the same level as genius, poets and the thinkers, whose sayings are judged from a purely aesthetic or philosophic point of view; and then, if the thing is well said, the man is a genius—and if it is unusually well said, then God said it!

In that way God is spirited away. What is he to do? If God stops a man on the road, and calls him with a revelation and sends him armed with divine authority among men, they say to him; from whom dost thou come? He answers: from God. But now God cannot help his messenger physically like a king, who gives him soldiers or policemen, or his ring or his signature, which is known to all; in short, God cannot help men by providing them with physical certainty that an Apostle is an Apostle—which would, moreover, be nonsense. Even miracles, if the Apostle has that gift, give no physical certainty; for the miracle is the object of faith. Moreover, it is nonsense to require *physical* certainty that an Apostle is an

Apostle (the paradoxical qualification of a spiritual relationship), just as it is nonsense to require a *physical* certainty that God exists, since God is *spirit*. The Apostle, then, says he comes from God. The others answer: Very well, then, let us see whether the content of your teaching is divine, in which case we will accept it, along with the fact that it was revealed to you. In that way both God and the Apostle are fooled. The divine authority of the one called should in fact be the sure protection which safeguards the teaching, and preserves it at the majestic distance of the divine from impertinent curiosity, instead of which the doctrine has to submit to being criticized and sniffed at—in order that people may discover whether it was a revelation or not; and probably in the meanwhile God and the Apostle have to wait at the gate, or in the porter's lodge, till the learned upstairs have settled the matter. The man who is called ought, according to divine ordinance, to use his divine authority in order to be rid of all the impertinent people who will not obey, but want to reason; and instead of that men have, at a single go, transformed the Apostle into an examinee who appears on the market with a new teaching.

What, then, is authority? Is it the profundity, the excellence, the cleverness of the doctrine? Not at all! If authority simply expressed in a higher potency, or reduplicated, the fact that the doctrine is profound, then there is no such thing as authority; for in that case if the learner were to assimilate this doctrine completely and entirely through the understanding, then there would cease to be any difference between the teacher and the learner. Authority is, on the contrary, something which remains unchanged, which one cannot acquire even by understanding the doctrine perfectly. *Authority is a specific quality which, coming from elsewhere, becomes qualitatively apparent when the content of the message or of the action is posited as indifferent.* Let us take an example, as simple as possible, where the situation is nevertheless made clear. When a man with authority says to a man, go! and when a man who has not the authority says, go! the expression (go!) and its content are identical; aesthetically it is, if you like, equally well said, but the authority makes the difference. If authority is not 'the other' (τò ἕτερον),* if it is in any sense merely a higher potency within the identity, then there is no such thing as authority. If a teacher is enthusiastically conscious that he has expressed the doctrine which he is proclaiming at the sacrifice of all else, this consciousness may well give him determination, but it does not give him authority. His life as a proof of the rightness of the teaching is not 'the other' (τò ἕτερον); it is

---

* Perhaps it will occur to some readers, as it occurs to me, to recall in connexion with this examination of 'authority' the 'Edifying Discourses' of Magister Kierkegaard, where he stresses the fact so clearly, by repeating word for word on each occasion, that 'they are not sermons, because the author is without authority to preach'. Authority is a specific quality either of an Apostolic calling or of ordination. To preach simply means to use authority; and that is exactly what is completely and utterly forgotten in these times.

a simple reduplication. The fact that he lives according to the doctrine does not prove that it is right, but only that because he is convinced of the righteousness of his teaching he therefore lives according to it. On the other hand, whether a police official is a rascal or an upright man—as soon as he is on duty he has authority.

In order to throw more light on the concept authority, so important for the sphere of the paradox-religious, I will elaborate the dialectic of authority.

Authority is inconceivable within the sphere of immanence, or else it can only be thought of as something transitory. In so far as one may speak of authority in political, social, and disciplinary connexions, or of using authority, authority is only a transitory factor, a passing thing which either vanishes later in time, or vanishes in so far as time and earthly life are transitory factors which disappear with all their differentiations. The only difference which can be *conceived* as the basis for the relations between man and man *qua* man is the difference within the identity of immanence, that is to say essential equality. The individual man cannot be *conceived* as differing from all other men by a specific quality (otherwise all thought would cease, as in fact it quite consistently does in the sphere of paradox-religion and of faith). All the human differences among men *qua* men vanish before thought as factors within the whole and within the quality of identity. For the moment it is my duty to respect and obey the difference, but religiously I may feel myself edified by the certainty that the differences disappear in eternity, those that single me out no less than those which weigh me down. As a subject it is my duty to honour and obey the king with undivided heart, but religiously I may feel strengthened by the thought that, essentially, I am a citizen of heaven and that should I ever meet the king after death I shall no longer be bound to him by the ties of obedience of a subject.

Such is the position as between man and man *qua* man. But between God and man there is an eternal, essential, qualitative difference which cannot, at the risk of presumption, be allowed to disappear in the blasphemous thought that, though certainly different in the transitory moment of time, so that man ought to obey and to pray God in this life, nevertheless the difference will, in eternity, vanish in an essential identity, so that in eternity God and man, like king and servant, become equals.

Between God and man, then, there is and remains an eternal, essential, qualitative difference. *The paradox-religious relationship* (which, quite rightly, cannot be thought, but only believed) *appears when God appoints a particular man to divine authority,* in relation, be it carefully noted, to that which God has entrusted to him. The man thus called is no longer related as man to man *qua* man; his relationship to other men is not that of a qualitative difference (such as genius, exceptional gifts, position, &c.), he is related paradoxically by having a specific quality which no immanence can resolve in the equality of eternity; for it is essentially paradoxical and *after* thought (not before, anterior to thought), contrary to thought. If a man thus called has a doctrine to bring forth according to a divine command, and another man, let us suppose, of himself and by himself discovered the same thing: then in all eternity the two things would not become equal; for the first man is different from every other man by virtue of his paradoxically specific quality (divine authority), and different from the immanently essential equality which is at the basis of all other human differences. The qualification 'an Apostle' belongs in the transcendental sphere, the sphere of paradox-religion which, quite consistently, also has a qualitatively different expression for the relation of other men to an Apostle: namely, they are related to him in faith, whereas thought is and breathes and has its being in immanence. But faith is not a transitory qualification, any more than the Apostle's paradoxical qualification was transitory. Between man and man *qua* man, then, no *established* or continuous authority was *conceivable*; it was something transitory. But for the sake of the essential consideration of authority, however, we may dwell for a moment upon a few examples of so-called, and in temporal conditions true, forms of authority. A king, it is assumed, has authority. Nevertheless, there is something disturbing in the idea of a king who is witty or an artist. The explanation of this is, surely, that one naturally lays the stress on his royal authority and so by comparison looks upon the more general human marks of distinction as something transitory, as something fortuitous, inessential and disturbing. A government department is regarded as having authority within its orbit. And yet it would be disturbing if its ordinances were really clever, witty, and profound. Here again the explanation is that, quite rightly, all the accent falls qualitatively on the authority. To ask whether a king is a genius—with the intention, if such were the case, of obeying him, is in reality *lèse-majesté;* for the question conceals a doubt as to whether one intends to submit to authority. To be prepared to obey a government department if it can be clever is really to make a fool of it. To honour one's father because he is intelligent is impiety.

However, as has already been said, between man and man *qua* man authority, when it exists, is something transitory, and eternity does away with all forms of worldly authority. But now, with regard to the transcendental sphere, let us take an example, as simple as possible and for that very reason as striking as can be. When Christ says, 'There is an eternal life'; and when a theological student says, 'There is an eternal life': both say the same thing, and there is no more deduction, development, profundity, or thoughtfulness in the first expression than in the second; both statements are, judged aesthetically, equally good. And yet there is an eternal qualitative difference between them! Christ, as God-Man, is in possession of the specific quality of authority which eternity can never mediate, just as in all eternity Christ can never be put on the same level as essential human equality. Christ taught, therefore, with authority. To ask whether Christ is profound is blasphemy, and is an attempt (whether conscious or not) to destroy Him surreptitiously; for the question conceals a doubt concerning His authority, and this attempt to weigh Him up is impertinent in its directness, behaving as though He were being examined, instead of which it is to Him that all power is given in heaven and upon earth.

Yet, nowadays, it is seldom, very seldom, that one hears or reads a religious discourse which is framed correctly. The better among them often dabble a little in what one might call unconscious or well-meant rebellion, by defending and upholding Christianity with all their strength—with the wrong categories. Let me take an example, the first that comes to hand. I prefer to choose a German because then I know that no one, not even the most stupid, not even the most wrong-headed, could imagine that I am writing about a matter which in my belief is infinitely important—in order to point to some clergyman or other. Bishop Sailer,* in a homily for the Fifth Sunday in Lent, preaches on the text John viii. 47–51. He chooses these two verses: 'He that is of God heareth God's word,' and 'If a man keep my sayings, he shall never die,' and continues: 'in these words of the Lord three great mysteries are solved, mysteries over which

---

* J.M. Sailer, 1751-1832, Bishop of Regensberg, tutor of Ludwig I of Bavaria.

men have racked their brains from the beginning of time'. There we have it. The word 'mystery', and particularly the 'three great mysteries', and then in the next phrase, 'over which men have racked their *brains*', immediately leads one's thoughts on to the profound in an intellectual sense; pondering, searching, speculation. Yet how can a simple apodictic statement be profound, an apodictic statement which is only what it is because so and so has said it; a statement which is not to be understood or fathomed, but simply believed? How can any man imagine that a mystery is solved, in a learned speculative way, by a direct statement, by an assertion? The question is, after all: Is there an eternal life? The answer: There is an eternal life. What, in heaven's name, is profound about that? If Christ had not said it, and if Christ was not who He said He was, then if the statement itself is profound, it must be possible to discover its profundity. Let us take the example of Herr Petersen, the theological student, who also says, 'There is an eternal life.' Would it ever strike any one to tax him with profundity on account of a direct statement? The decisive thing is not the statement, but the fact that it was Christ who said it; but the confusing thing is that, as though in order to tempt people to believe, they talk about profundity. In order to speak correctly a Christian priest would have to say, quite simply: We have Christ's word for it that there is an eternal life; and that settles the matter. There is no question here of racking one's brains or philosophizing, but simply that Christ said it, not as a profound thinker but with divine authority. Let us go further, let us suppose that a man believes in eternal life on Christ's word. In that case he believes without any fuss about being profound and searching and philosophical and 'racking his brains'. On the other hand, take the case of a man who racks his brains and ruminates profoundly on the question of immortality: would he not be justified in denying that this direct statement is a profound answer to the question? What Plato says on immortality really is profound, reached after deep study; but then poor Plato has no authority whatsoever.

In the meanwhile, the thing is this. Doubt and superstition, which make of faith a vain thing, have among other things also made men shy of obedience, of bowing before authority. This rebelliousness worms its way even into the thought of better people, perhaps unbeknown to them, and so begins all the extravagance, which at bottom is only treachery, about the profundity and the beauty which one can but faintly perceive. And so if one had to describe the Christian-religious discourse as it is now heard with a single definite predicate, one would have to say it was *affected*. Normally in referring to a priest's affectation, one means the way he dresses, or gets himself up, or that he talks in a sugary voice, or that he rolls his Rs like a foreigner, wrinkles his brow, or uses violent gestures and ridiculous poses. All this, however, is of less importance, though it is desirable that he should not do so. But the pernicious thing is when the whole train of his thought is affected, when the price of its orthodoxy is an emphasis in an entirely wrong place, when he calls for faith in Christ, when he preaches faith in Him on grounds which simply cannot be the object of faith. If a son were to say, 'I obey my father, not because he is my father but because he is a genius, or because his orders are always profoundly intelligent,' then that filial obedience is affected. The son accentuates something entirely wrong, he emphasizes the intellectual aspect, the profundity in a *command*, whereas a command is, of course, indifferent to that qualification. The son wishes to obey by virtue of the father's intellectual profundity; and to *obey* by virtue thereof is just what is not possible, for his critical attitude as to whether the command is profound undermines the obedience. And so, too, it is affectation to speak of adopting Christianity and believing Christ because of the great profundity of the doctrine. By putting the accent in entirely the wrong place one only makes a show of orthodoxy. The whole of modern philosophy[*] is therefore affected, because it has done away with *obedience* on the one hand, and *authority* on the other, and then, in spite of everything, claims to be orthodox. A priest who is quite correct in his discourse would, when quoting the words of Christ, have to speak in this way: 'These words were spoken by Him to whom, according to His own statement, is given all power in heaven and on earth. You who hear me must consider within yourselves whether you will

---

[*] Contemporary—i.e. Hegel.

bow before his authority or not, accept and believe the words or not. But if you do not wish to do so, then for heaven's sake do not go and accept the words because they are clever or profound or wonderfully beautiful, for that is a mockery of God.' For, once the command of authority, of the specific paradox-authority, is posited, then all relationships are qualitatively changed, then the kind of acceptance which was previously allowable and desirable becomes a crime and presumptious.

But now how can an Apostle prove that he has authority? If he could prove it *physically*, then he would not be an Apostle. He has no other proof than his own statement. That has to be so; for otherwise the believer's relationship to him would be direct instead of being paradoxical. In the transitory conditions of authority between man and man *qua* man, authority will normally be physically recognizable by power. An Apostle has no other proof than his own statement, and at the most his willingness to suffer anything for the sake of that statement. His words in this respect will be short: 'I am called by God; do with me what you will, scourge me, persecute me, but my last words are my first: I am called by God, and I make you eternally responsible for what you do against me.' Let us suppose that an Apostle were really to have power in the worldly sense, had great influence and powerful connexions, the forces with which one is victorious over men's opinions and judgements—then if he used them he would *eo ipso* have lost his cause. By using power he would have defined his efforts as essentially identical with those of other men, and yet an Apostle is only what he is through his paradoxical heterogeneity, through having divine authority, which he can possess absolutely and unchanged even if he is looked upon by men, as St. Paul says, as less than the filth they walk upon.

(3) *Genius has only an immanent teleology; the Apostle is absolutely, paradoxically, teleologically placed.*

If a man can be said to be situated absolutely teleologically, then he is an Apostle. The doctrine communicated to him is not a task which he is given to ponder over, it is not given him for his own sake, he is, on the contrary, on a mission and has to proclaim the doctrine and use authority. Just as a man, sent into the town with a letter, has nothing to do with its contents, but has only to deliver it; just as a minister who is sent to a foreign court is not responsible for the content of the message, but has only to convey it correctly: so, too, an Apostle has really only to be faithful in his service, and to carry out his task. Therein lies the essence of an Apostle's life of self-sacrifice, even if he were never persecuted, in the fact that he is 'poor, yet making many rich', that he never dares take the time or the quiet or carefreeness in order to grow rich. Intellectually speaking he is like a tireless housewife who herself hardly has time to eat, so busy is she preparing food for others. And even though at first he might have hoped for a long life, his life to the very end will remain unchanged, for there will always be new people to whom to proclaim the doctrine. Although a revelation is a paradoxical factor which surpasses man's understanding, one can nevertheless understand this much, which has, moreover, proved to be the case everywhere: that a man is called by a revelation to go out in the world, to proclaim the Word, to act and to suffer, to a life of uninterrupted activity as the Lord's messenger. But that a man should be called by a revelation to sit back and enjoy his possessions undisturbed, in active literary *far niente,* momentarily clever, and afterwards as publisher and editor of the uncertainties of his cleverness: that is something approaching blasphemy.[*]

It is otherwise with genius; it has only an immanent teleology, it develops itself, and while developing itself this self-development projects itself as its work. It thus receives importance, perhaps even great importance, but it is not teleologically situated in regard to the world and to others. Genius lives in itself; and, humorously, might live withdrawn and self-satisfied, without for that reason taking its gifts in vain, so long as it develops itself earnestly and industriously, following its own genius, regardless of whether others profit by it or not. Genius is therefore in no sense inactive, and works within itself perhaps harder than a dozen business men put together, but none of its achievements have any exterior *telos.* That is at once the humanity and the pride of genius: the humanity lies in the fact that it does not define

---

[*] A reference to Mag. Adler.

itself teleologically in relation to any other man, as though there were any one who needed it; its pride lies in the fact that it immanently relates itself to itself. It is modest of the nightingale not to require any one to listen to it; but it is also proud of the nightingale not to care whether any one listens to it or not. The dialectic of genius will give particular offence in our times, where the masses, the many, the public, and other such abstractions contrive to turn everything topsy-turvy. The honoured public, the domineering masses, wish genius to express that it exists for their sake; they only see one side of the dialectic of genius, take offence at its pride and do not perceive that the same thing is also modesty and humility. The honoured public and the domineering masses would therefore also take the existence of an Apostle in vain. For it is certainly true that he exists absolutely for the sake of others, is sent out for the sake of others; but it is not the masses and not mankind and not the public, not even the highly educated public, which is his lord and master—but God; and the Apostle is one who has divine authority to command both the masses and the public.

The humorous self-sufficiency of genius is the unity of a modest resignation in the world and a proud elevation above the world: of being an unnecessary superfluity and a precious ornament. If the genius is an artist, then he accomplishes his work of art, but neither he nor his work of art has a *telos* outside him. Or he is an author, who abolishes every teleological relation to his environment and humorously defines himself as a poet. Lyrical art has certainly no *telos* outside it: and whether a man writes a short lyric or folios, it makes no difference to the quality of the nature of his work. The lyrical author is only concerned with his production, enjoys the pleasure of producing, often perhaps only after pain and effort; but he has nothing to do with others, he does not write *in order that:* in order to enlighten men or in order to help them along the right road, in order to bring about something; in short, he does not write *in order that*. The same is true of every genius. No genius has an *in order that;* the Apostle has absolutely and paradoxically, an *in order that.*

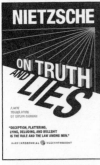

ISBN 978-0-06-171869-4

ISBN 978-0-06-156161-0

ISBN 978-0-06-176631-2

ISBN 978-0-06-155024-9

ISBN 978-0-06-176521-6

ISBN 978-0-06-163265-5

ISBN 978-0-06-176824-8

ISBN 978-0-06-187599-1

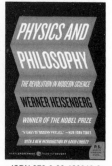

ISBN 978-0-06-120919-2

Available wherever books are sold, or call 1-800-311-3761 to order.